Y0-ALL-025

PATHWAYS THROUGH THE JEWISH HOLIDAYS

PATHWAYS THROUGH THE JEWISH HOLIDAYS

by
SULAMITH ISH-KISHOR

edited by
Benjamin Efron

KTAV PUBLISHING HOUSE, INC.

Design and art supervision by EZEKIEL SCHLOSS

**chapter drawings by
Stuart Diamond**

Copyright 1967

Ktav Publishing House, Inc.
New York, New York 10002

All rights reserved. No part of this book may be reproduced in any form
without permission in writing from the publisher.

Library of Congress Catalog Card No. 67-18815

Manufactured in the United States of America

TABLE OF CONTENTS

- 3   Holidays in the United States
- 9   Rosh Hashanah—Yom Kippur
- 25   Sukkot—Simchat Torah
- 37   Chanukah
- 53   Tu Bish'vat
- 59   Purim
- 72   Pesach
- 87   Yom Haatzmaut
- 95   Lag BaOmer
- 101   Shavuot
- 109   Shabbat
- 121   Tishah B'Av
- 127   Yom Hazicaron
- 131   Looking Back Over The Holiday Year
- 136   Index

HOLIDAYS IN THE UNITED STATES

A. Science and God

In this day of scientific development, people begin their thinking while still very young.

You think about space flight, you think about computing machines, you think about a future world where people might be living out in space, or under the water of lake or sea, in formerly ice-frozen wilderness or formerly impassable jungles. You think about surgery that makes and replaces human organs.

You think that the time may come when mankind will create machines that will not only do the work of people, but that will seem to *be* people.

Perhaps this makes you feel very far from God, or even doubt that there is a divine Creator, since we human beings seem able to imitate nature so well.

But remember this: Norbert Wiener, the inventor of the computer, said, "My machine may be able to answer every question. But it can never *ask* a question." No machine can ever do more than arrange material that is put into it first by man's mind and hand.

No matter how marvelously human-like a machine may be, it took a created man-mind to make it.

Even if future research discovers what seems to be the secret of life, and is able in some degree to make a living thing—it still will take a created man-mind to do it.

And where did that created mind come from?

Albert Einstein, one of the greatest of human minds, said this: "Throughout all my researches, I have always felt myself to be upon the trail of a vast Intelligence."

In other words, he knew that reason, science, research, did not disprove but rather

The Statue of Liberty in Paris, France.

suggested that there is in the universe an order which could not have come about by mere coincidence. Many scientists accept the idea of the existence of a Creator of all things, whom we call God.

Religious people believe God created mankind as well as everything else on earth, and that He did so because He wanted to. In the Hebrew Bible it says that God was pleased with His handiwork, and that man was given the job of making the world a good place to live in. Jews believe that God intended people to aim at becoming the best human beings possible. Each one should help to make life worthwhile for everybody.

This is the real purpose and meaning of the Jewish faith, and the real meaning behind our Law; the meaning which we bring out in all our Jewish observances and "holy" days: "What is hateful to thyself, do not do unto thy fellow-human."

B. Americans Have Many Holidays

The Statue of Liberty in the harbor of New York has become so well known that many of us have forgotten its original intention. "Liberty" holds up a torch, to mean that freedom of the people enlightens the world.

The statue was sent us by the French nation in 1876 to celebrate the hundredth anniversary of America's Independence Day, July 4th. This holiday reminds the world that America was established as a land of liberty to which people of all races and creeds might come.

And they did come: people from other parts of the world, people of older nations, different religions, other colors, various ways of thinking.

As each group arrived, settled down, and became American citizens, the immigrants grew more and more like the rest of the people in their ways of thinking and their habits of living.

Yet the people of each group loved their old ways and customs; they held on to many of them, particularly those which they enjoyed, or which had special meaning. So they kept their old-time holidays. But at the same time they began to observe American holidays, too. The more American they became, the more they grew to love these holidays which they now celebrated together with their neighbors.

March 17th is by this time almost an American holiday, especially in New York City,

Saint Patrick's Day parade in 1874 in New York City.

St. Patrick's Day parade in New York City.

where there are so many Americans of Irish descent. Every New Yorker knows that on this day a broad green line is painted down the middle of Fifth Avenue, and traffic there is stopped, while thousands of Irish-Americans march up the road, all wearing a bit of green in honor of the country of their origin. There is some kind of celebration on March 17th in every large American city where any considerable number of Irish people have settled.

This day is called St. Patrick's Day because he is the patron saint of Ireland. Long ago, in Ireland, it was much more of a religious holiday, but nowadays in America, it is really a get-together day for Irish-Americans, when they sing the old Irish songs, tell the old Irish legends, and recall the struggles of the Irish people for freedom.

Each national group in America, in fact, has a special holiday. One day you may see an amusing procession wearing quaint costumes from old-time Germany, another day a colorful parade of Spanish-American citizens, or a gay Italian fiesta in the streets where Italians live, when the houses are strung with lights and the people march carrying brightly painted figures of their saints, singing and praying as they go.

On September 16th in Los Angeles, California, Mexican-Americans hold a parade in honor of Mexican Independence Day. And in Chinatown, about January 10th, New Yorkers can see the Chinese celebrating their New Year, with parades and mock fights of fantastic paper dragons and lions.

In New Orleans, one of the oldest cities in America, there are many Americans of French descent, who brought the celebration known as "Mardi Gras" (Shrove Tuesday) to America. It is a time of gay festivities that date back two hundred years to the days when France still had kings. "Mardi Gras" began as a religious holiday, or rather as the last day of normal living before the long Lenten fast, when for six weeks observant Christians refrain from amusements and give up eating some accustomed foods.

Mardis Gras float in New Orleans.

Americans of Czechoslovak background celebrate Jan Hus Day to honor their religious leader, who was put to death centuries ago because he refused to give up his religious beliefs.

There are also Jewish holidays that have become a part of American life wherever there are large numbers of Jews. It is impossible for people of other religions not to notice that numerous stores are closed on *Rosh Hashanah* and *Yom Kippur,* and that on these days, in cities like New York, the theatres, movies, sports and concert halls are half empty because so many Jews spend most of those days in the synagogue.

The children of all these different groups therefore have two kinds of holiday: their own religious and historical ones, plus the national American days such as Lincoln's Birthday, Washington's Birthday, Independence Day, Labor Day, Columbus Day, and Veterans' Day. The latter are holidays for the whole American nation; schools and banks and many government offices are closed.

Wherever people live, there are national holidays which celebrate events the people want to remember. In addition, each religious group has its own days of religious observance.

C. Holidays Do Change

As times change, conditions change; some of the past is forgotten and new events create new occasions for remembrance. Sometimes people forget the reason and purpose of a holiday because it had its beginning such a long time ago. Or the life of the country they live in changes so much that the holiday has to change.

For example, countries ruled by a king usually keep the king's birthday as a holiday. When a king dies, the date of the birthday

Thirteen veterans of the Union Army marched in the 1937 Memorial Day Parade.

celebration has to be changed for that of the new king. Sometimes a government sets an official "birthday" for its monarchs, to prevent the date of the holiday from changing. In England, for instance, the official birthday is June 2, perhaps because they can hope for good weather at that time!

When a country stopped being a monarchy and became a republic, the people generally wanted to honor the day on which this change took place, and the new government of course did not wish to celebrate the king's birthday any more. Often they made a holiday of the birthday of the first President, as America did after it became a republic. Then there would be two holidays where there used to be one: an Independence Day, as with America's July the Fourth, and the first President's birthday, as with George Washington.

An interesting example of a holiday that changed in our own time is Veterans' Day.

On November 11, 1918 at about 11 A.M., factory whistles blew, bells pealed, cannons were fired and a wave of wild rejoicing swept over the United States. The First World War was over! Germany had surrendered! The Kaiser had left his throne and had gone to chop wood in Holland for the rest of his life. Our soldiers were coming home! By evening people were dancing in the streets. In New York, all traffic stopped while everybody celebrated. The day was declared a legal holiday.

The following year and every year thereafter the people celebrated November 11th as Armistice Day, the day that the Allies and the leaders of the enemy agreed to stop shooting at each other. On that day our war veterans went out on the streets of America to sell red poppies made of paper or linen. Everybody bought at least one because the money was going to the Veterans' Hospitals for our wounded.

Years later, from 1939 to 1945, there was the Second World War, longer and far more terrible. This war did not end on November 11th, but we did not give up observing that day as Armistice Day. It had become an accepted American custom during the twenty-seven years of its history, since 1918. No new holiday was declared in honor of the end of the Second World War. We simply went on observing Armistice Day, only we began to call it Veterans' Day. In this way November 11th stood for the end of both world wars.

Even after 1945, veterans continued to sell the poppies. People, however, were not quite sure why. The reason lay in the war of 1914-1918. An English poet, killed in Flanders during that war, had written a poem, asking that the war be carried on until victory against the brutal enemy was finally won.

*If you break faith with us who die,
We shall not sleep, though poppies grow
In Flanders' fields.*

The poppy had no special meaning in World War II, but artificial poppy selling had become so well established as a custom connected with November 11th that it continues to be part of Veterans' Day. This kind of thing happens with many holidays; customs remain long after anyone remembers why.

One day, we hope, there will be no more wars, and perhaps we will then change Veterans' Day to Peace Day. If people in that hoped-for day still continue to sell red poppies, it will not be for veterans' hospitals, but for peaceful activities. And if, at that time, the question is asked, "Why red poppies?" we may have to give a new explanation because the old one would no longer be understood.

This has also happened to some religious holidays. Sometimes we want to keep a custom of the holiday, but the old reason may not fit the times. In that case, we work out new reasons, and they are usually just as acceptable. Our Jewish holidays have also undergone change, which makes them very interesting to read about, as you will soon see.

Armistice Day celebration at Arlington National Cemetery.

ROSH HASHANAH YOM KIPPUR

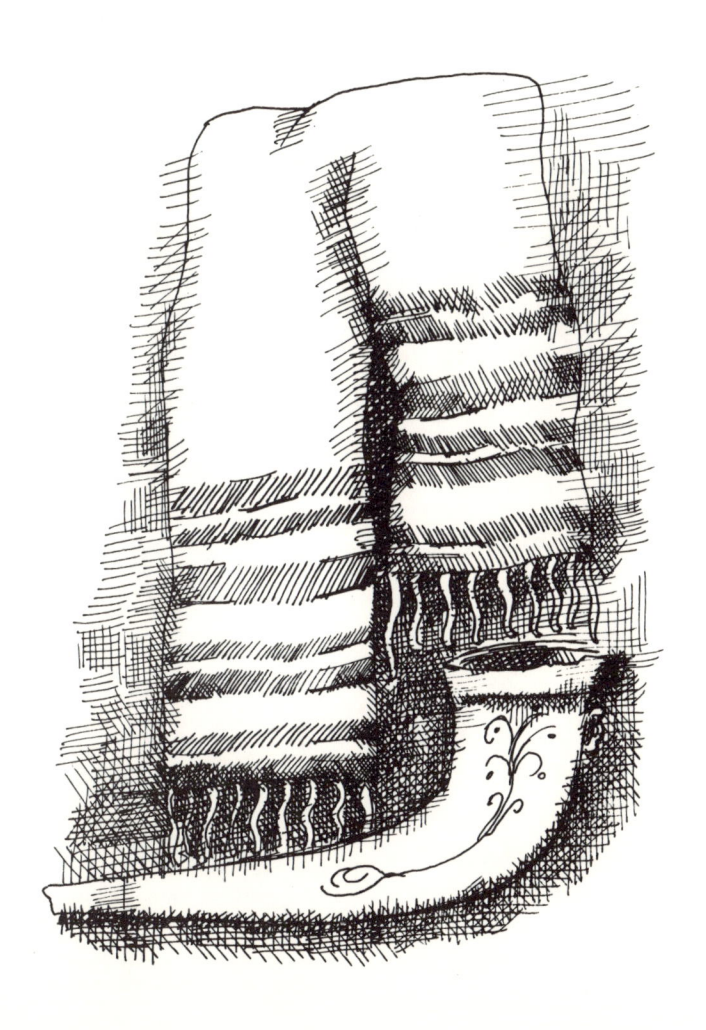

A. When Is a New Year?

The first thing your non-Jewish friend may ask, when you tell him in September that this is your New Year's holiday, is this:

"How come your New Year's Day is in the fall? Why don't Jews have New Year on January first, the way everybody else does?"

First of all, you can tell him, everybody else *doesn't*.

The Chinese people, with one of the oldest civilizations in the world, have their New Year some time in the middle of January. The Russian old-time religious New Year comes about the 12th of January. The Mohammedan New Year comes in springtime.

In ancient times, the people of Babylon and the people of Persia began their New Year in the spring. The ancient Egyptians felt that the New Year came when the River Nile began to rise and fertilize their land, which was in the summer. The ancient Romans began the New Year in the winter,

The earliest recorded Jewish calendar (and earliest Hebrew inscription) is this 10th-century B.C.E. clay tablet found near Gezer, Israel. Written by a farmer in ancient Hebrew script, the Gezer Calendar lists the agricultural seasons and the work associated with them.

Two sample pages from a Hebrew calendar. Notice the variety of information.

which is probably where the western world took it from, as they also took the Roman alphabet and much of the Roman law.

The Hebrews who lived in the ancient land of Palestine decided, for their own good reasons, that their year ended with the gathering-in of the harvest at the end of summer, and therefore the New Year began at that time. They worked hard and long in the fields and in the vineyards, for their whole future depended on whether the harvest was good or poor, so they felt as if the old year had not really ended until the result of their work was known.

B. What Is the Date?

If you asked an American Jew when the State of Israel celebrated its eighteenth year of Independence, he would be right if he said April 25, 1966. But if you asked an Israeli, he would say Iyar 5, 5726. It seems odd that there should be such a difference in the year, 1966 and 5726.

But it's not hard to explain. Leaders in the Christian or Western world decided to count the years of history from the time Jesus, whom they called the Lord, the son of God, was born. The year of his birth became the year One A. D., standing for "Anno Domini" (in the year of the Lord). Any event *after* the birth of Jesus was dated accordingly. The year of our Declaration of Independence, for example, was 1776 A. D., 1776 years after Jesus was born.

For the events of history that had occurred *before* Jesus's birth, they counted backwards. For example, the death of Julius Caesar took

11

place forty-four years before the birth of Jesus. Christians therefore called the date 44 B. C. ("Before Christ"). Christ is not a name but a word meaning Messiah.

The Jewish people, in existence long before Christianity developed, had been counting history from the time of Creation. In the Jewish calendar the year of Jesus's birth was 3760. For religious reasons, they could not accept the Christian system since they would then have to use "Anno Domini," which refers to Jesus as the Lord. The Jews recognize only God as the Lord. Nor could they accept B.C. (Before Christ), for that would be acknowledging that Jesus was the promised Messiah, which Jews do not believe. Jews therefore went right on counting past 3760 and so we are now, according to the Jewish calendar, in the Hebrew years 5727, 5728, etc.

Practically, however, we have had to follow the dating of the Western world, except that we have changed the initials. For events *after,* we say C. E. (the Common Era), and for happenings *before,* we say B. C. E. (*Before the Common Era*). Thus it is 44 B. C. E. for the death of Julius Caesar and 1776 C. E. for the Declaration of Independence. (A general rule for arriving at the Hebrew religious date is to add 3760 years to the Christian or Western date.)

If you should ask a Chinese boy what year it is according to the ancient Chinese system, he would give quite a different answer. And a Mohammedan boy, in figuring the year according to *his* religion, would subtract 622 from the Western date, because Mohammedans count the years of *their* calendar from the year 622 C. E., when their prophet Mohammed made an important religious journey. 622 is their Year One.

No one way of dating is the "right" one. It is really a matter of custom and accepted

A design in the floor of a synagogue built at Bet Alpha in the sixth century C.E. There are signs of the zodiac, Jewish symbols, and inscriptions in Hebrew, Greek and Aramaic. This shows that the Jewish community in Palestine was still strong although Babylonia was the main center of learning.

tradition. Careful records are kept by historians in every civilized country, thus the date for an event in one system can be equated with the date given for the same event in any other system.

C. Calendars, Calendars, Calendars

We know from scientific measurements and mathematics that it takes the earth three hundred sixty-five and one-quarter days to go around the sun. The modern Western world bases its calendar on this journey around the sun, counting 365 days to the year. For three years we forget about the extra quarter of a day, but in the fourth year we equalize our reckoning by adding one day to the short month of February, making that year 366 days long.

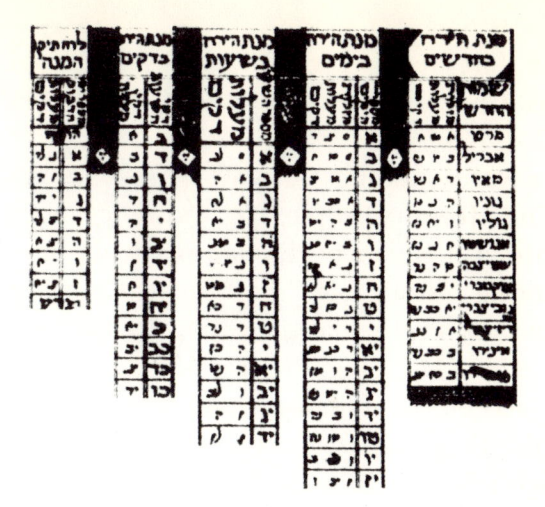

In the very early world, before it was known that the earth goes around the sun, people counted days and seasons by the moon. (The Mohammedans still do so.) Shepherd tribes, which the Jews once were, who led their herds from one grassy field to the next, found it natural to figure the passage of time by the moon because they could actually see how it changed. First, a dark, moonless night when it seemed that the moon might never come back. Then, oh joy! the faint, narrow silvery curve appeared in the sky—a new moon!

The ancients felt that this was a cause for thanks and celebration, as if the almighty power that ruled the skies was being good to them by bringing the moon back. So the time of the new moon became a time of rejoicing and worship in the ancient world.

This Hebrew Almanac, prepared by the Jewish astronomer Abraham Zacuto, was used by Christopher Columbus on his voyage to the New World. With it Columbus predicted an eclipse of the moon.

A Chasidic Jew in Jerusalem, Israel, stands beneath a sundial awaiting the arrival of the Sabbath.

Also, since the changing of the moon occurred regularly, it became a natural way of counting the days and months. But when the Jewish shepherd tribes settled in Palestine and became farmers too, they found that they had to know when the seasons began and ended so they could plant and tend their crops at the proper time.

The seasons, however, depended on the sun. There were times when it was very warm for a number of months, and periods when it turned too cool for proper growing. But those people who counted time by the moon found that it was not always the same lunar month when the warm weather or the rainy season came. (A lunar month refers to the 29½ days from one new moon to the next. The word comes from Latin, "luna," the moon.)

Why was this? It was because twelve lunar months totaled only three hundred fifty-four days, and this did not equal the twelve months of the sun year, which totalled three hundred and sixty-five and one-quarter days. The eleven day difference could throw all their reckoning off, for after three years of

JEWISH CALENDAR

f Fast day

TISHRI	(September-October)
1	Rosh Hashanah
2	Rosh Hashanah, Second Day
1–10	The Ten Days of Penitence
3	Tzom Gedaliah f
10	Yom Kippur f
15	Sukkot (9 days—15th–23rd)
16	Sukkot, Second Day
17–21	Chol Hamoed of Sukkot
21	Hoshanah Rabbah
22	Shemini Atzeret
23	Simchat Torah

CHESHVAN   (October-November)

KISLEV   (November-December)
25 Chanukah (8 days—25th of Kislev—2nd of Tevet)

TEVET   (December-January)
2 Last Day of Chanukkah
10 Asarah Betevet f

SHEVAT   (January-February)
15 Chamishah Asar Bishvat

ADAR   (February-March)
13 Taanit Esther f
14 Purim
15 Shushan Purim

VEADAR   added in leap years (March-April)
13 Taanit Esther f
14 Purim
15 Shushan Purim

NISAN   (March-April)
14 Taanit Behorim f
15 Passover   (8 days—15th–22nd)
16 Passover, Second Day   1st of the 50 days of Omer (or Sefirah)
17–20 Chol Hamoed of Passover
21 Passover, Seventh Day
22 Passover, Eighth Day

IYAR   (April-May)
18 Lag B₀Omer   33rd day of Omer

SIVAN   (May-June)
6 Shavuot, First Day   End of the 50 days of Omer (Sefirah)
7 Shavuot, Second Day

TAMMUZ   (June-July)
17 Shivah Asar Betammuz f

AV   (July-August)
9 Tishah B'av f

ELUL   (August-September)

A Jewish holiday calendar for the complete year.

moon counting, the difference could amount to more than a month. In nine years, the difference would be more than three months; the date for spring planting would actually arrive, according to the moon-calendar, in the dead of winter!

They therefore had to find a way to equalize the moon-time with the sun-time. Someone eventually figured out that the two systems of counting could be equalized over a period of nineteen years. A regular pattern was developed whereby the Jews doubled the last Hebrew month (*Adar*), calling it "Adar the Second," every third, sixth, eighth, eleventh, fourteenth, seventeenth and nineteenth year.

It was a clumsy method of equalizing the two ways of counting, but when you realize how little science even the best mathematicians knew in that far-off time, thousands of years ago, you can see that it was quite an ingenious plan for them to have thought out. For it worked so well that the Hebrew calendar is still equalized in this way.

So a child of that time had to learn, among other things, which year it was of the 19 year cycle before he could tell when his birthday came!

According to the Bible the order of the Hebrew months was as follows:

1, *Nisan;* 2, *Iyar;* 3, *Sivan;* 4, *Tammuz;* 5, *Av;* 6, *Elul;* 7, *Tishri;* 8, *Cheshvan;* 9, *Kislev;* 10, *Tevet;* 11, *Shevat;* 12, *Adar.*

This is the order of the Hebrew months today too. We should therefore—let's face it—really have *two* New Years! There should

14

be one at the start of the first month in spring, Nisan, for the Bible actually tells us to consider this the first month of the year. But we do not have a special New Year's holiday for it; hardly any one thinks of it as the first of the Hebrew year.

The first day of Tishri is the day on which the Jews observe the beginning of the year. We call it by the Hebrew name of Rosh Hashanah (the "head" of the year). This day has been observed by the Jews for many centuries, although Tishri is actually the seventh month. Our tradition even has it that the creation of the world began on the first day of Tishri.

D. High Holidays in Temple Times

It is not known exactly how the New Year was observed in ancient times. It was not until after the destruction of the Temple of Solomon that the first of Tishri was formally celebrated as Rosh Hashanah, with the blowing of the *shofar,* with special hymns describing God as the judge of all humanity, and with prayers for forgiveness of sins.

The High Priest, in the days the Temple still stood, played a very important part in these services, especially on Yom Kippur. He was not permitted to sleep the night of *Erev Yom Kippur;* many other Jews also kept awake, praying and reading psalms. The High Priest underwent a ceremonial bath at the Temple before he put on the special robes for the daily sacrifice. He also wore a golden crown, the priestly breast-plate with twelve jewels (one for each of the Twelve Tribes of Israel), and golden bells on the hem of his robe.

A reconstruction of Herod's temple in Jerusalem.

A reconstruction of the regalia of the Cohanim.

After the regular morning service, he bathed again, changed the ceremonial robes for simple white linen, and prepared for the special Yom Kippur service. During the service in the "Holy of Holies," the Inner Sanctuary, he pronounced the name of God in its most sacred form. When he called it out, the congregation bowed down to the ground and hid their faces.

Another ancient custom seems to have been the choosing of a goat to bear all the sins of the people. The Hebrews of early Biblical times probably believed that by a special ritual and ceremony they could transfer their sins to the animal. The goat was then driven out of the city into the wilderness, a red ribbon tied to its horns. This was the "scape goat" that was supposed to leave the people free of sins. No doubt some people realized that this was only a symbol indicating that they were ashamed of their sins and wanted to get rid of them. In addition, another goat was sacrificed to God.

The High Priest changed garments and bathed a number of times on Yom Kippur, once for each different part of the day's observances. This bathing signified purification. At evening, when all the prayers and chants and ceremonies of the day were over, the people broke their fast and there was celebration and feasting in Jerusalem.

E. In the European Ghetto

Pious Jews all over the world, when they no longer had the holy Temple in Jerusalem, tried to recreate in their lives the spirit of the ancient observances of the Hebrews. Living in hardship, especially in Eastern Europe, where there was great poverty, the Jews nevertheless showed strong religious feeling. In fact, it was the *practice* of Judaism that gave

A reconstruction of the Holy of Holies of the Temple in Jerusalem.

Tzedakah—charity, is a virtue especially associated with the High Holy Days. This beautifully crafted silver tzedakah box was made in Germany in 1880.

the High Holy Days it was decided who was to live and who was to die, who was to be happy and who was to have sorrow in the next year.

In the ghetto sections of East European towns many years ago, the *Shamash* (the Rabbi's helper) made the rounds of the streets late at night during the week before Rosh Hashanah, knocking on the windows and calling the families of the town to come to the synagogue. These late services were referred to as *S'lichot* (prayers for forgiveness), which prepared the people for the solemn days that were coming.

On Rosh Hashanah morning the services began very early. About mid-day came the sacred moment for the blowing of the shofar. From the most ancient times, the shofar was blown to proclaim important events and to announce religious occasions. The Torah spe-

pleasure and meaning to their lives. So, when Rosh Hashanah and Yom Kippur drew near, the people began to prepare their minds for the High Holy Days. They tried to be more considerate of others, and asked people to forgive them for any slight or hurt they might have been guilty of during the year. They prayed more often, they studied the *Torah* more, and recited the Psalms more fervently. They gave more money to charity, and went to cemeteries to visit the graves of their families.

Even young children felt they must be more quiet and obedient, for they, too, believed the time was coming when every one, themselves and their parents and teachers, was going to be judged in Heaven. The children knew the Jewish belief that during

Service for Yom Kippur by Jewish troops in the German army encamped near the city of Metz in 1870.

"O King who sits on His throne of rightousness." This page of S'lichot (repentance) prayers is from a nineteenth century European High Holiday prayer book.

Jews performing the *Tashlich* ceremony. Woodcut, Augsburg, Germany, 1531. The woodcut represents Jewish men and women casting their sins into the river.

cifically tells us, as a matter of fact, to observe the first day of Tishri with the blowing of the shofar. It has become such an important Jewish symbol that our ancestors believed the final Day of Judgment would be announced by the archangel Gabriel blowing the shofar.

During the day pious Jews walked to the nearest stream or river, where they threw in some crumbs of bread while saying prayers. This ceremony is called *Tashlich* (casting out), from a verse in the biblical Book of Micah, the prophet, who prayed that the Lord would cast all the sins of the Jews into the depth of the sea.

On the tenth day of the month of Tishri, the most solemn day of the Jewish calendar, Yom Kippur (the Day of Atonement) was observed with a full day's total fast. Late in the afternoon of the day before, the East European Jewish family ate a special holiday meal to make sure that their strength would last through the next twenty-four hours without eating or drinking. Then they went off to the synagogue. On Yom Kippur the women wore white dresses (if they had them) and the men put on white robes and prayer shawls.

The great moment of the Yom Kippur Eve service was, as it still is, the singing of the *Kol Nidre* (All the Vows), a prayer in which pardon is asked for all unfulfilled vows and promises made to God. It is a very sad, beautiful and haunting melody. Worshippers sometimes weep during the chanting of this prayer.

The Jews modeled many of their Yom Kippur rituals and ceremonies on those performed in the Temple at Jerusalem many centuries before. That is why the Jews of the East European ghettos used to prostrate them-

A shofar is made from the horn of a ram. The above is a German shofar from the year 1782.

Page with the *Kol Nidre* prayer, from a Jewish-German Machzor printed at Cracow, Poland, 1571.

F. Times Change

Today, in modern America and all over the Western world, life is very different and the observances of religion have been taking on different forms.

In the autumn of 1966, the last day of the Hebrew month Elul fell on the American date of September 14th. The next day, September 15th, was the first of Tishri, Rosh Hashanah.

A few thousand years ago, in Jerusalem, they would have sent out messengers to watch for the rising of the new moon in the sky, then runners would have been dispatched to announce to outlying Jewish communities that Elul was over and Tishri, the New Year month, had begun. But suppose that night turned out to be cloudy and no moon could be seen. The Jews would have been afraid

selves on the ground during one part of the services, hiding their faces, as was done in old Jerusalem when the High Priest of the Temple went into the Holy of Holies and called upon the name of God.

After a day of almost continuous prayer and lament, came the *N'ila* (closing), when it was believed the Book of Judgment was closed in heaven. Those who truly repented their sins were believed to have been inscribed for a good New Year; the rest would suffer the punishment they deserved. The congregation, rising, listened to a last blast of the shofar. Yom Kippur was over.

Silver plate with artistically engraved shofar-blowing scene. Persian, nineteenth century.

This map shows the points at which signal fires were built to announce the beginning of the new month. Starting at Jerusalem, the message was sent to the cities of Babylonia, so that all Jews would keep the holidays at the same time.

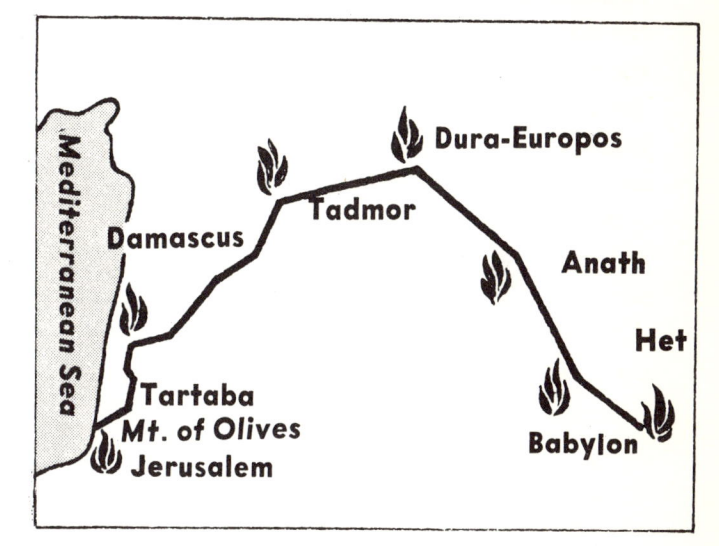

to wait for the next night to check up, because then they would not be certain as to which was the right day to observe as Rosh Hashanah. Maybe they should have observed it the day before! The custom therefore grew

Rosh Hashanah kiddush.

up in ancient times to celebrate an extra day for each holiday, to make sure they would observe it in time.

Today, however, we do not have to see the new moon with our own eyes. Our knowledge of science makes it possible to tell exactly when the new moon is supposed to appear, and so we know exactly when to start the holiday. Many Jews therefore began to feel that it was no longer necessary to devote two days to Rosh Hashanah. They decided to observe it for only one day.

The Orthodox Jew of modern times sticks as closely as possible to the religious forms that developed in Eastern Europe. These were patterned after the ancient observances of Israel in the days of the Temple. But Reform Jews believe they can retain everything that is really important in the Hebrew faith without following every ritual of the past. For instance, in most Reform synagogues the wearing of the skullcap, the white robe, or the prayer shawl has been discontinued.

A family that follows Reform Judaism will come together for a holiday meal before the Erev Rosh Hashanah service. This is like a Friday night supper in an observing Reform household. A *Kiddush* is said or chanted, and the *brachah* (blessing), is said over the *challah*, the holiday white twist bread.

At Rosh Hashanah there is probably a bowl of honey on the table, and each one at the table dips a piece of challah into it, to express the hope that life in the New Year may be sweet and pleasant.

For the Reform congregation, also, the exciting moment in the service on Rosh Hashanah is the sounding of the shofar. The congregation, too, looks forward to the New Year's sermon the rabbi delivers, and for the younger children there is a special service at which the shofar is also blown.

There is a certain amount of cheerfulness at Rosh Hashanah, in keeping with the hopefulness of Judaism. People dress up for attendance at the synagogue, and there is a holiday feeling in the air. But there is also a strong feeling of solemnity, for Rosh Hashanah is a time to be thoughtful, a time to think over

The Bible says, "In the seventh month, on the first day of the month, shall be a solemn rest to you, a memorial proclaimed by a blast of horn . . ."

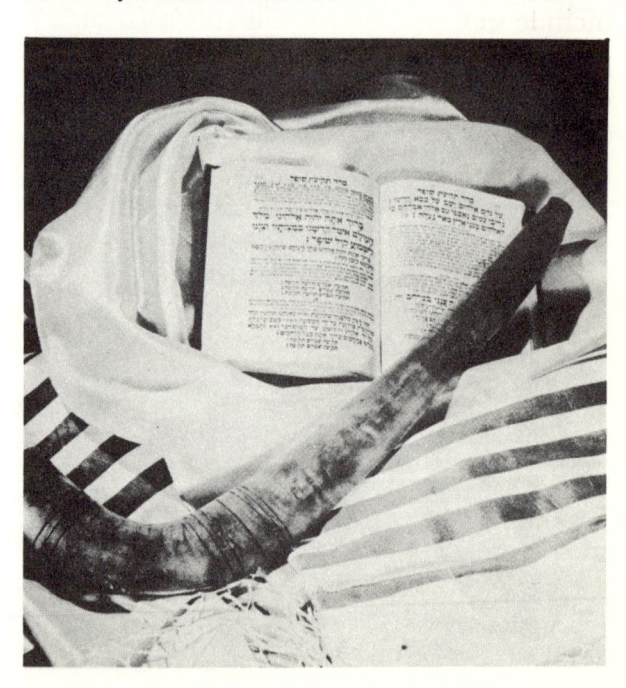

The Temple choir beautifies the High holiday services.

the deeds of the past year. In Judaism there is always time to make up for every unkindness, every act of inconsideration or rudeness, every wrong we have committed.

Much more solemn is the Holy Day of Yom Kippur. In most Reform families, the Yom Kippur fast begins at sunset, and for twenty-four hours no one (except young children) is supposed to eat or drink. (This does not include sick people, for the Jewish religion provides that any observance may be suspended if a person's health is threatened.) Sometimes younger children insist on fasting for at least part of the time, so that they, too, can feel "in on it."

The most moving experience of the Erev Yom Kippur service is still the singing of the Kol Nidre. During the services of the following day, memorial prayers known as *Yizkor* (Remembrance) are said for the dead. There is also a special prayer called *Al chet schechatanu* (For the sin we have sinned), which is recited by the whole congregation. A great many sins are mentioned in this prayer which the people read aloud together; some of the wrongdoings we ourselves may be innocent of, but naming them aloud reminds the whole congregation that these acts are against the teachings of Judaism.

The prayer is recited by all for another reason too. Judaism is the religion of a people, the people of Israel. The whole congregation, therefore, confesses all the sins that any of its members may have committed, and seeks pardon for the whole congregation.

Yom Kippur closes with the N'ila service and the blowing of the shofar about the time of sunset, and the congregation then goes off to break its fast.

G. The Holy Days in Modern Israel

In the modern State of Israel, the High Holidays are observed in a slightly different mood. The synagogues there are as crowded

The Rabbi explains the meaning of the High Holy Days to a young worshipper.

21

An Israeli soldier blows a Yemenite shofar during services in a field.

as in America, but Rosh Hashanah is also a time for the Israelis to visit their relatives and friends.

In Israel the length of the Jewish holidays is dictated by the Bible. Passover, for instance, is celebrated for seven days, not for eight as the tradition-minded Jews do everywhere else. What the Bible says about the first day of Tishri indicates that Rosh Hashanah should be observed for only one day. The strong tradition of two days for Rosh Hashanah which the people who settled Israel brought with them evidently caused the founders of modern Israel to keep it as a two-day holiday. This decision gives the people more time to travel and visit.

And do they *go!* Travel all over Israel at the Rosh Hashanah period is so heavy that the inter-city buses (called *Egged*) have reported carrying as many as a million passengers to and from Jerusalem!

New immigrants who arrive in Israel just before the Holy Days are rushed to their new homes so they can celebrate their first holiday in comfort. With what joy, what fervor such new settlers enter into the spirit of the New Year! To many of them, just being in Israel is sufficient happiness; they do not even need honey and wine to make their New Year seem sweet!

The President of Israel attends synagogue in Jerusalem. Hundreds of shofars are distributed to the armed forces and special services are conducted for soldiers on duty.

Schools, of course, are closed. Millions of greeting cards go back and forth among the Israelis, and to and from friends and relatives in other lands.

Because in Israel the High Holidays are part of the State religion, the members of the diplomatic corps in Israel come to visit the President and pay their respects.

As for the very Orthodox Jews of Israel, some of whom are descendants of ancient Palestinian families who never left the soil, they

Tashlich ceremony in Israel along the Mediterranean Sea.

22

worship according to ancient customs as much as possible. If you visit there and see them going barefoot on Yom Kippur, it is because they abstain from all comforts on that day. Watching them, one could imagine oneself back in olden times. As in America, the old lives on beside the new.

H. An Observance from a Far-Off Land

Being scattered among other nations, it is inevitable that Jews should acquire varying customs and habits, even in their religious observances.

Most striking is the difference in the attitude which the Jews of Persia maintain in regard to Yom Kippur. They consider the confession of sins and errors as a cause for gladness. It brings forgiveness and peace and a happier relationship with one's neighbors, one's relatives, and with God, provided that it is sincere and that one tries to make up for past wrongdoing and unkindness. They send each other flowers and good wishes for the holiday.

They also believe that one should not be afraid of God's judgment, that He will judge them as a loving father would judge his children, severely, but for their own good. While the prayers are being said, they sit in comfort, the children play, they all rejoice because they can start a New Year with clean hearts.

The belief of the Persian Jews that Yom Kippur should be a day of comfort and happiness, rather than of grief and awe, is not without basis. For on Yom Kippur certain psalms are sung or chanted, and one of them, sung just before Kol Nidre, says:

*There shall be light for the righteous,
And gladness for the upright in heart.*

They take this to mean that those who confess their sins and strive not to do wrong in the future, who try to make up for any wrong or hurt they did in the past year, will be rewarded with lightness of heart. And this is true. Anybody who has ever done a real kindness, or made it up to someone for harm done him, knows what wonderful lightness and joy this brings to the heart.

A fifteenth century Spanish High Holiday prayer book. In case of a surprise raid by the Spanish Inquisition, this elongated book could easily be hidden inside the folds of their wide sleeve.

HEBREW HOLIDAY TERMS

ROSH HASHANAH

Rosh Hashanah	רֹאשׁ הַשָּׁנָה	the start of the New Year
l'shanah tovah tikatevu	לְשָׁנָה טוֹבָה תִּכָּתֵבוּ	may you be written down for a good year
shofar	שׁוֹפָר	a ram's horn
Tishri	תִּשְׁרֵי	Tishri, the month of Rosh Hashanah

YOM KIPPUR

Yom Kippur	יוֹם כִּפּוּר	Day of Atonement
Kol Nidre	כָּל נִדְרֵי	All the vows (famous prayer)

SUKKOT | SIMCHAT TORAH

A. When, Why and How

Sukkot is one of the most delightful holidays that any people ever had.

It is a happy time, a time of satisfaction in having finished the work of the season, a time to enjoy the fruits, vegetables and grains that the earth has brought forth. It was a harvest festival in ancient Israel lasting eight days, and it is that again today.

Long ago, when the Jews were dependent on the crops for their existence, Sukkot was one of the most important festivals of the year. It began, in fact, as a nature festival. Other nations also made a holiday of harvest time, and prayed to whatever gods or goddesses they believed had power over their fields. Jews honored the God of Israel, the One God they called the Creator of the universe. They traveled in caravans to the sanctuaries where they could worship Him, each bringing what he could for the sacrifice. It might be a fine sheep, an ox or a goat. Or the poor might bring only a jar of grain or a skinful of wine.

Israel is world-famous for its excellent wines. Here the grapes are being gathered in giant barrels.

An Arab family gathering their harvest in the same manner as their forefathers, thousands of years ago. In the foreground is a *sukkah* built of branches and leaves to provide shade from the hot afternoon sun.

Sukkot was a time for singing and dancing and drinking of wine. People gathered in large crowds and set up tents and booths, and this was pleasant after long months on lonely farms and grazing-meadows. It is not surprising that a lot of them overdid the celebrating, and sometimes behaved in ways that were not quite fitting for a religious festival.

In later times, however, the prophets and other religious leaders disapproved of the wildness of the festivities at Sukkot and tried to persuade the people to behave properly.

A time came when the Torah and the Ten Commandments became the constitution of the Jewish community. Some other changes were then introduced into the festival. The people still built booths, but the reason given for continuing this custom underwent a change. People said it was to commemorate the forty years of wandering in the wilderness with Moses, when the Hebrews had to live in temporary tents and huts. This helped give a more serious tone to the holiday, and in time solemn prayers were incorporated into the service for Sukkot.

In very ancient times, however, the emphasis was upon the nature aspects of the holiday.

Sukkot had some solemn moments then too. On the last day of Sukkot, which is called *Shemini Atzeret* (the eighth day of assembly), there were special sacrifices and prayers. Since the life of the whole people in those days depended on having sufficient rain, the most important part of the service on this day was a prayer for rain.

The *sukkah* (meaning tent or booth) was regarded as a symbol of God's protection of Israel. There were definite instructions in ancient times as to how it was to be built. It was not to be higher than twenty cubits (a cubit is about a foot and a half), and not lower than ten times the breadth of a man's hand (about seven inches). For if it were very high, it would express pride, and if it were too low, if would be miserly and uncomfortable.

The four kinds of growing things: *etrog, lulav, hadassah* and *aravah.*

It was to be more in the shade than in the sun; this was to show the virtue of restraint and humbleness, rather than an eagerness to be noticed. The roof had to be latticed, and covered only partly with leaves and branches, so that at night the stars might be seen. This was because the stars would draw the eye up to heaven. Fruits and vegetables were to be hung within, as a reminder of the harvest which God gives us out of the earth.

There are differing ideas as to the reasons for choosing the *etrog, lulav, hadassah* and *aravah* as symbols to represent the four kinds of growing things. One of the explanations for the four symbols is that mankind is composed of four sorts of people:

One, the learned and religious;

Two, the learned who do not observe the Law;

Three, those who are not learned but who do good and are honest;

Four, those who are neither learned nor good.

The first are represented by the etrog (citron), for it has both a pleasant taste and a delicious fragrance.

A second or third century C.E. engraved Jewish tombstone with a menorah flanked by the "four kinds."

The second are represented by the lulav (palm branch), for its fruit can be eaten but it has no fragrance.

For the third we have the hadassah (myrtle), which has fragrance but cannot be eaten.

And for the fourth there is the aravah (willow), which cannot be eaten and has no fragrance.

It is interesting to note that other people beside the Jews regarded the willow as a symbol of grief and loss. In many folk-songs and poems of the English people, for instance, the word "willow" is used as a sad refrain.

During the Sukkot services the four symbols were used, and the lulav was pointed in all directions to indicate God's rule over the whole earth. At the end of the festival, in olden times, the branches were beaten on the ground till all their leaves fell off, to show that the old harvest was over and that they prayed for a new harvest next year.

Another explanation for beating off the leaves of the lulav, hadassah and aravah is that it proved people had not carelessly forgotten the sins of the past year, even though Yom Kippur was over. By beating off the leaves they showed their desire to shake off any sins that might still have been in their hearts.

B. In Temple Times

Sukkot was one of the three great holidays of the year when every Jew who could possibly make the journey went to Jerusalem to join the celebration.

Most people traveled in groups and families, or in great caravans of scores and hundreds of people. Some rode on camels or donkeys, but it was considered more righteous to travel on foot. The great Rabbi Hillel was said to have left his home in Babylonia and to have walked the whole way, a distance of several hundred miles!

It was very exciting, especially for those who came to Jerusalem for the first time. It

A photograph of the ancient walls of Jerusalem. If only these giant stones could talk! What tales they could tell!

must have been like our coming from a small town to see New York. But it was even grander, for Jerusalem was the holy city, where stood the great Temple.

At Sukkot time, Jerusalem's towers, roofs and courtyards, even the streets, were filled with branches and fruits so that the city looked like one vast garden. Everybody seemed to be going toward the Temple, for on the first day of Sukkot a procession formed for the special water-ritual. This was very important, for it was believed that on Sukkot

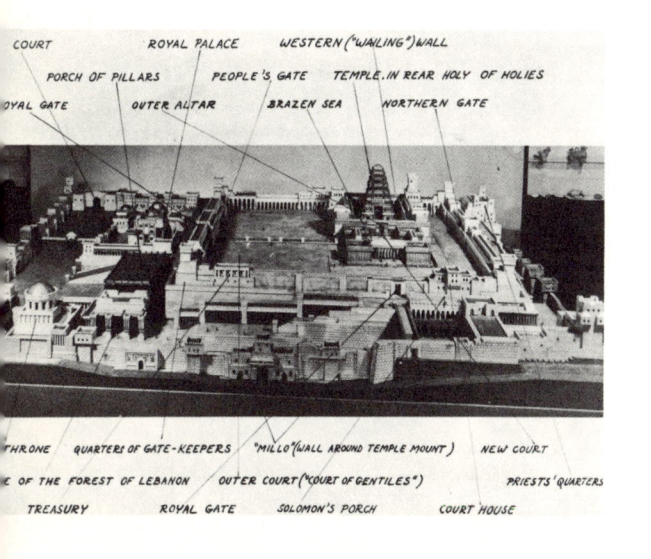

A reconstruction of Solomon's Temple.

Pool of Hezekiah in Old City of Jerusalem. King of Judah, 720-692 B.C.E. He fortified Jerusalem and built the Siloam tunnel to improve the city's water supply.

God made the decision whether or not to send the rainfall on which the country's life depended.

The priest took a golden pitcher and led the people down the mount to the spring of Siloam. There everybody watched while he filled the pitcher with water; then they followed him back to the Temple, through the Water Gate, where more crowds waited. Priests blew silver trumpets while others sang songs of rejoicing. Around the altar stood lines of other priests waving willow branches. They poured water from the golden pitcher onto the altar, and the choir sang psalms of praise to God. Then all the people, waving their palm branches, joined in the words, "We beseech Thee, O Lord, to save us and to make us prosper."

This ceremony brought great satisfaction, for it gave the people hope that God would remember their need for plentiful rain.

A reconstruction of the bronze altar of the Holy Temple.

In the evening there was ceremonial dancing at the Temple. The men carried lighted torches which they tossed up and caught as they danced, while musicians played harps, cymbals, flutes and other musical instruments.

The same ceremonies took place every day, but on the seventh day the priests marched round the altar seven times and beat their willow branches on the earth. That evening the regular daily sacrifice was watched with great attention by the people, for they believed that they would be able to tell, from the direction in which the smoke blew from the fire on the altar, whether there would be a good rainfall. They hoped it would blow to the east, for this, they believed, meant rain, a good harvest, and prosperity to come.

C. Sukkot in the East-European Ghetto

Many things changed for the Jewish people when the Second Temple was destroyed, but Sukkot remained a pleasant and joyful holiday. The building of the sukkah, eating meals in it, carrying out ceremonials connected with the fruits and branches, always made it different and exciting.

In Europe, especially in Eastern Europe, observant Jews tried to keep as much as possible of the ancient ceremonies. Whatever could no longer be actually done, such as marching around the holy altar, they did in a symbolic way, making their procession inside the synagogue.

Everybody helped in building the sukkah for the family. Sometimes families got together to make a communal sukkah. Since the etrog had to be imported into Europe, it was expensive; not many people could afford to buy it, so several families or groups would get together to purchase one etrog.

As there were always many poor Jews in the community, an etrog was made available at the synagogue to be used by everyone who needed it.

The poor were also invited to eat in the sukkot of the well-to-do. A poor guest would be regarded as doing his host a favor, for part of the ritual of the holiday required the head of the household to bring the needy into the sukkah in keeping with God's commandment to feed the hungry.

An early paper flag for *Simchat Torah* shows King David kneeling. The text: "David rejoiced on *Simchat Torah*."

A father and son in Chasidic costume recite the blessing over the *lulav* and *etrog*.

Etrog (citron) container, made in Germany about 1860. The etrog lies in the box when it is not in use.

During the centuries of exile from Palestine, when the Jewish people were often very cruelly treated in the various countries of Europe, their need for help in saving them from persecution and destruction was very real. Their prayers went up to God from hearts full of fear and grief, and when a holiday brought the people closer to God they let their sorrow pour forth from them in heartfelt praying or weeping. At times this happened on Sukkot, on the day known as *Hoshanah Rabbah,* when seven trips around the altar were made.

This seems to be out of keeping with the spirit of Sukkot as a time for rejoicing in the harvest. But the Jews of Europe were not shepherds or farmers any longer. Unfriendly laws had forced them off the land. While they still thought of Sukkot as an agricultural festival, they had already become accustomed to connecting it more with the forty years of wandering in the desert, after the deliverance from Egypt. They liked to think of the sukkot as the temporary huts the ancient Hebrews set up during those years in the wilderness. Perhaps some of the sadness came from

A pewter plate (Germany, 19th century) depicts a Sukkot scene taking place in a synagogue.

31

The first sentence in the book of Genesis: "In the beginning God created the heaven and earth." From a Bible printed in Prague in 1518. Only two copies of this book are in existence.

their longing to be able to live freely as Jews, the way the ancients did in the time of Moses.

The greatest moment of the Exodus was the giving of the Torah at Mount Sinai. There was such love for the Torah among Jews, a day was added to the festival to express the joy of the people at having been chosen to receive the Torah. The added day was given the name of *Simchat Torah* (Rejoicing in the Law). On that day the scrolls of the Law were taken out of the Ark and carried around the synagogue. People of the congregation lovingly touched the scrolls with the fringes of their prayer shawl, or stroked the covering in reverence as the scrolls passed by.

And the Torah reading on that day was something special. The rabbis wanted people to understand that the study of Torah must never end, it must not even *seem* to stop. They therefore arranged the readings so that on Simchat Torah the last verse of the Book of Deuteronomy would be read and would be followed immediately by the reading of the first verse of the Book of Genesis. Simchat Torah thus symbolizes the continuousness of Torah reading and study; it marks the close tie between the Jewish people and the laws of God.

D. Sukkot in Modern America

Sukkot begins to be real for most American Jewish children when, just four days after Yom Kippur, they see the beautifully decorated sukkah (or tabernacle) at the synagogue.

The fresh scent of the branches that form its roof and walls, the bright colors of the fruits and vegetables hanging from the roof and sides, are truly exciting. Children love to see the bunches of ripe grapes, green or purple, the scarlet tomatoes, the yellow and red corn; to many it is a reminder of the farms they have seen in the countryside. The members of Reform congregations, like other syn-

The fragrance and color of Indian corn, fruits and vegetables remind us of the beauty of the harvest. Young and old help decorate the sukkah.

American soldiers celebrating Sukkot at an overseas base.

agogue-going Jews, enjoy coming to the temple sukkah after services in order to recite the kiddush there. Seeing the sukkah makes clearer to the children why the ancient Sukkot prayers thank God for the harvest of the past year, and why they ask Him to send a plentiful rainfall the following year, so that a new harvest may grow and ripen.

Perhaps some of us think of rain in our big cities as a nuisance, interfering with baseball or football games, causing colds or spoiling picnics and camp or scout cookouts. But we must remember that nothing, even in our days of scientific know-how, can take the place of rain on our orchards and grain-fields. Without sufficient rain, everything withers and dries up; even America's rich soil would produce little without it. When reservoirs do not fill up, water for drinking, cooking and washing may run short. Fires start very readily during long, dry spells, and are hard to put out.

So we can understand, even today in the cities, the need and hope for rain. And so Jews who celebrate Sukkot in America include these special prayers for rain.

Reform Religious Schools make a gay festival of the holiday of Sukkot. Members of the Sisterhood or Youth Group decorate the sukkah built in the courtyard of the temple, hanging within it in artistic manner whatever can be found in the market of autumn fruits and produce. A table is festively set with a holiday cloth, a large challah, candlesticks, fruits, and greens. Care is taken to provide the sukkah with the four traditional symbols of the holiday, the lulav, etrog, aravah and hadassah. For while Reform Jews have introduced new ideas into Sukkot, they do like to return to the meaningful customs of olden times. And these four fruits of the earth—palm branch, citron, willow and myrtle—represent the four species of plant life.

The children are usually called in groups, during religious school sessions, to come into the sukkah to say the *brachot* of the holiday and to eat and drink within its festive walls.

A Sukkot table with a giant challah and candlesticks. The boy is about to recite the blessing over the *lulav* and *etrog*.

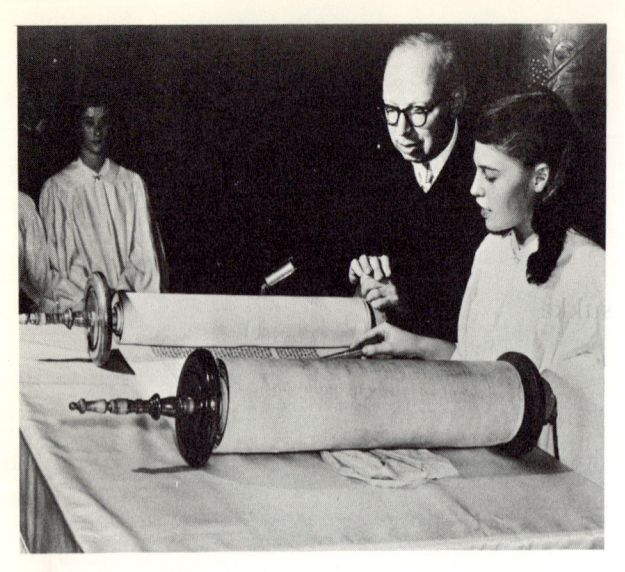

The Rabbi and his students read the Torah.

Reform Jews observe Sukkot for eight days. They combine into one day the observance of Shemini Atzeret and the celebration of Simchat Torah. For Shemini Atzeret there is a Yizkor (Memorial) service for the departed, but for Simchat Torah there is a joyful spirit and much gaiety. The Torahs are taken out of the Ark and are carried by a grandfather and son and grandson around the sanctuary, followed by the congregation. They join in singing happy songs as the procession winds many times around the large hall. The children usually carry bright Simchat Torah flags, or in some places miniature Torahs, as they join the gay *hakafot* (processions). They receive apples and other goodies after the service, in honor of the Torah which was given us as a guide for our life.

Most Reform congregations perform a special ceremony of Consecration on the last day of the holiday. During the service, when the last verses of Deuteronomy and the first verses of Genesis are read, the Rabbi calls up all the children who are new in the Religious School, to give them a special blessing. This ceremony is made part of the Torah reading, and the new students are in this way given their first *aliyah* (going up to the Torah).

The temple usually gives each consecrant a miniature Torah as a memento of the occasion.

It is a colorful and exciting week, and everyone is sorry when it is over. The frame of the sukkah looks bare when the fruits and branches and produce are taken out, but there is always the hope that there will be another sukkah next year.

E. Modern Israel Celebrates

Sukkot, as it is celebrated in the State of Israel today, combines many ceremonials of the past with some new customs that have come out of the life of the Israelis in recent times.

In some respects modern Israel looks like ancient Palestine at Sukkot time. There are home-made tabernacles, covered with roofs of branches and leaves, on rooftops and balconies, and in courtyards and gardens; sukkot seem to spring up like mushrooms all over the city of Jerusalem.

A happy *hakafot* procession with flags and Torah.

In Israel one can find a sukkah in almost every back yard. Here we see a family putting the finishing touches.

The synagogues hold services during which the people carry the etrog and lulav, as in ages past, honoring Sukkot as a harvest festival. The drawing of water from the springs is carried out at home with singing and dancing, especially in the *kibbutzim* (collective settlements).

As it is very warm in Israel during the month of Tishri, thousands of Israelis go on trips and hikes. Some go on a "Peace Pilgrimage" to Mount Zion; seventy candles are lighted at this ceremony in substitution for the ancient peace-sacrifice of seventy bullocks, one for every nation then thought to exist in the world.

Simchat Torah is celebrated in Israel on the same day as Shemini Atzeret, for the people there observe the holiday for eight days too, as Reform Jews do in the United States.

The processions carrying the Scrolls of the Law go through the streets of the cities as well as inside the synagogues. In Jerusalem thousands of people gather to watch these hakafot being held near the synagogue of the Chief Rabbinate.

In the Orthodox Quarter musicians play old chassidic melodies on a balcony during the public circuits of the scrolls.

The local religious council of Tel Aviv sets up twelve entertainment centers in the various quarters. The elders of the Bokhar Quarter march in their embroidered robes, followed by congregants carrying the community's Torahs.

The young people of Haifa, with their bands gaily playing music old and new, march through the crowded streets in the Simchat Torah parade, organized by the National Religious Party in Hadar Ha-Carmel.

It is a thrilling moment when, at the now customary Simchat Torah reception by the President, Israelis pronounce the traditional blessing on seeing the head of State. For the first time in two thousand years the Jews are able to say this blessing for the head of a Jewish State!

Every Sukkot the Israelis hold a swimming contest. It is a three-mile course on the ancient Sea of Galilee, the beautiful Lake Kinneret. Twenty-five hundred swimmers entered in 5723 (1963). The winner was a girl, the Dutch champion Judith de Nijs. In a two-and-a-half mile course, a few days later, from Ein Geb to Tiberias, the winner was the Israeli champion, Gershon Shefa, with a record of two hours, six minutes and five-point-seven seconds. Miss de Nijs was second.

For Israeli Jews there seems to be a richer, more exultant feeling about a Sukkot festival, since they are farming the very same soil on which the ancient holiday was celebrated. They rejoice in the harvest at the very same time their forefathers did, and can celebrate under the same weather conditions. But even more important: Israelis are happy to have the chance, after so many centuries of being without land, once again to produce food for themselves from their own soil.

HEBREW HOLIDAY TERMS

SUKKOT

Sukkot	סֻכּוֹת	Festival of Booths
lulav	לוּלָב	palm leaf
etrog	אֶתְרוֹג	citrus fruit
sheheche-yanu	שֶׁהֶחֱיָנוּ	who kept us alive, blessing for start of a festival
yom tov	יוֹם טוֹב	holiday
Shemini Atzeret	שְׁמִינִי עֲצֶרֶת	Festival of the Eighth Day

SIMCHAT TORAH

Simchat Torah	שִׂמְחַת תּוֹרָה	Joy in the Torah
hakafot	הַקָּפוֹת	processions with the Torah
chag sameach	חַג שָׂמֵחַ	a happy festival

CHANUKAH

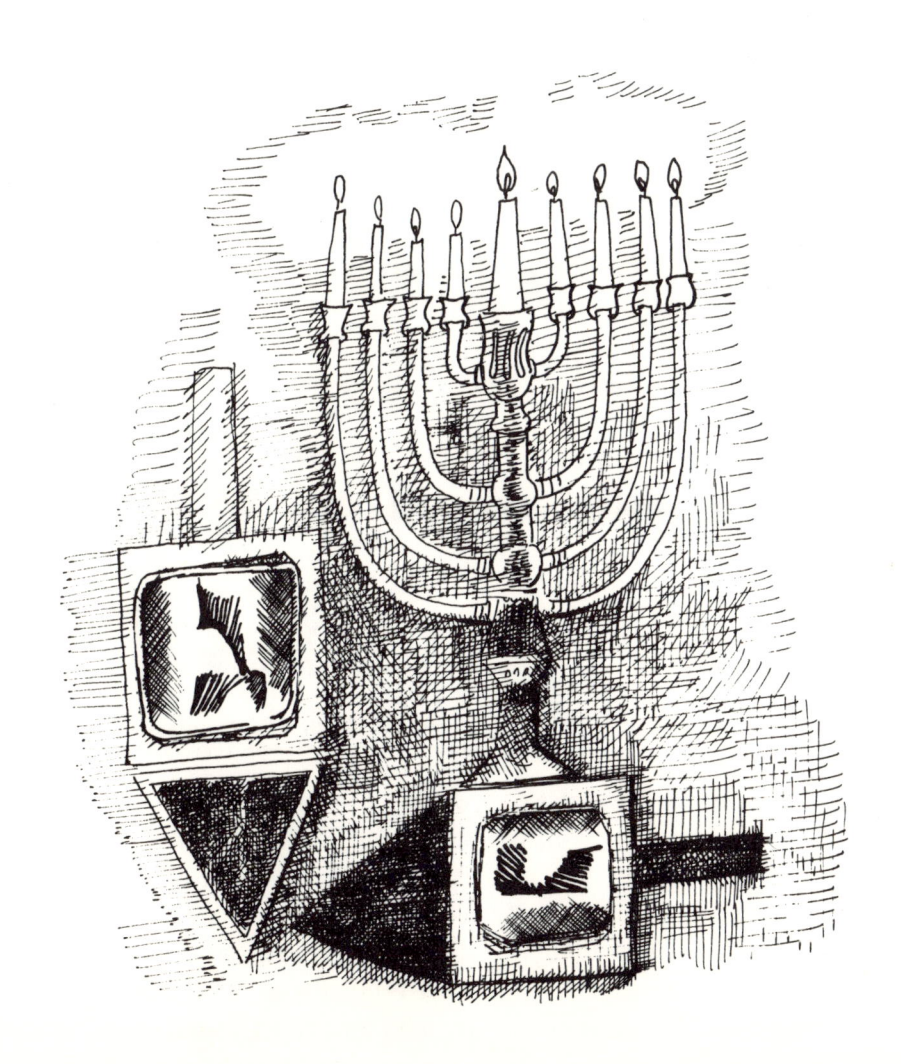

A. The First War for Religious Freedom

The festival of *Chanukah* begins on the twenty-fifth day of the Jewish month of Kislev, in winter, and lasts eight days.

On each of these nights, Jewish families all over the world light candles, one for the first night, two for the second, three for the third, and so on until there are eight candles burning, in addition to the shamash (helper) candle with which the counted candles are lit.

The real spiritual meaning of this ceremony is that the light of the Torah was renewed, and the light of religious liberty was kindled by the event which this holiday celebrates.

That is why the story of Chanukah is exciting and unforgettable.

It happened in 165 B.C.E.

Before then there was a period of comparative peace for the Jews. Their country had been conquered by the powerful Persian emperors who ruled over most of the known world, but the Jews were left in peace, to study the Torah and to follow its teachings. All they were asked to do was to pay taxes. A Persian governor lived in Jerusalem, but he did not really rule them. The Jews had their own High Priest, who was also their chief or prince, and represented them as a people.

Alexander the Great being greeted by the High Priest Jaddua. From a fourteenth century French picture.

Greek inscription carved on a synagogue column.

This peaceful time lasted about two centuries.

Then came Alexander the Great, the young, vigorous, brilliant general who, between 336 and 333 B.C.E. took over the Persian Empire including Palestine. He died shortly afterwards, and his empire was divided among his generals. Palestine fell into the hands of a Syrian-Greek family that tried to make all their people follow Greek customs and worship. This, the Syrian-Greek rulers felt, would keep the people they governed more loyal to them.

A small number of Jews, mainly the landowners, priests and merchants, did not mind changing their ways. There were advantages to be gained by going along with the Syrian rulers; business was good, and many Jews had become rich trading with other parts of the Syrian-Greek Empire. So they altered their Jewish names to Greek (even Joshua, the High Priest and Governor, called himself Jason). They wore Greek-style clothes and sandals, they began to speak Greek rather than Hebrew, and studied Greek philosophy.

But the really religious Jews, who cared more for their ancient heritage of Judaism, disliked all this "Hellenizing" (Hellas was the ancient name of Greece; its culture was called Hellenism). There were some things they liked about Greek life, but they saw beauty in their own customs and did not feel there was any reason why they should give up the traditions and practices that had come down to them.

Then Antiochus IV became ruler of the Syrian Empire, about the year 175 B.C.E. He became involved in wars in far parts of the Middle Eastern world. He decided to make all his subjects live according to his Greek ways, which he thought would prevent rebellions while he was busy fighting, and he demanded from the Jews, too, that they prove their loyalty to him by worshipping the Greek gods.

The other peoples under the rule of Antiochus didn't mind. They were accustomed to worshipping idols, to sacrificing in the way the Greeks did, so they were content to worship the Greek gods and to honor King Antiochus as a god. But when the Jews saw the Syrian-Greek officers bring idols into their holy Temple, and saw pigs being sacrificed on

Statue of Zeus (Jupiter) found at Caesarea. Throughout Judea, Syrian overlords pressed the Jews to worship before such idols at public altars.

39

Coin of Antiochus IV.

the holy altar, they were horrified. Then Antiochus ordered Jews to stop studying Torah, and to give up their observance of the Sabbath and other commandments.

There were many Jews who refused to endure it. They fled to the caves and the hills, and formed guerrilla bands to resist the Syrian-Greeks. The Syrian army tried to hunt them out; many Jews were caught and slain. But the caves of Israel are numerous, their openings are very low and narrow, hardly to be distinguished from the solid rock; inside they are large and can shelter many people. So the number of Jewish resistance fighters constantly increased.

And then one day in the town of Modi'in a man named Mattathias, member of a priestly family and father of five strong, grown sons, appeared in the town square at the command of Syrian-Greek officers. All the Jews of the area had been ordered to come there to worship at the specially constructed Greek altar. But, instead of bowing down to the Greek idol, Mattathias called upon the Jews to attack the Syrians, and then to follow him to the hills. Many Jews heeded his call. When he died, his son Judah, who was so strong that he was called *Maccabee* (the hammer), went forth and took up the leadership. Judah was a brilliant strategist; soon he and his guerrillas were driving the Syrian army before them.

In 165 B.C.E. they defeated the army of the Syrians, and were able to re-enter Jerusalem. They had won the right to worship in their own way and to live their life as Jews once again.

Rejoicing, they went to the Temple.

It was in a tragic condition, made unholy by the statues of Greek gods, neglected, dirty. But the people came, singing joyfully and

This is Modi'in, where, according to tradition, the heroic Maccabees are buried.

Two Maccabean coins.

with new hope. They rebuilt the altar and made new holy vessels. And on the 25th of Kislev they were ready to rededicate the Temple. Judah Maccabee then proclaimed an eight day holiday for the Chanukah (Dedication) of the purified Temple.

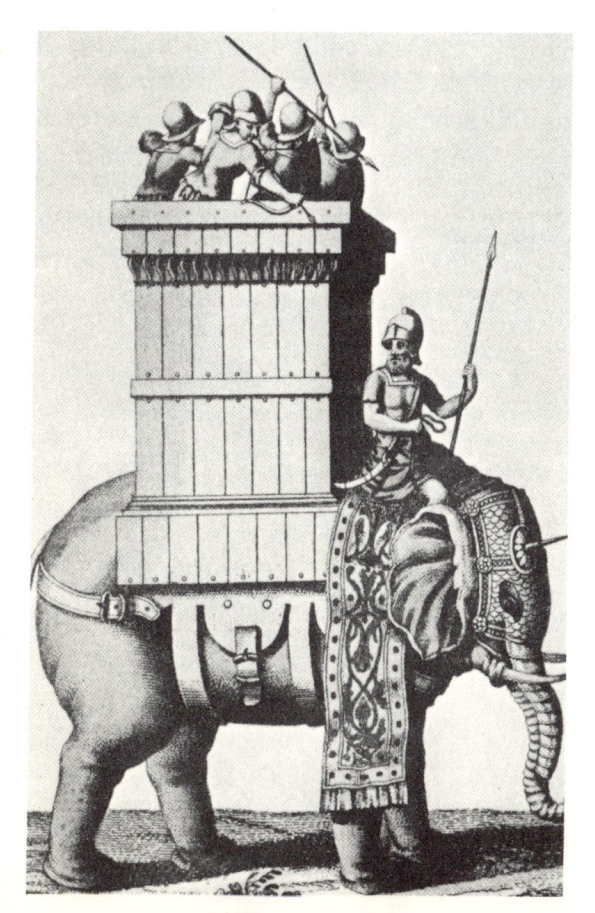

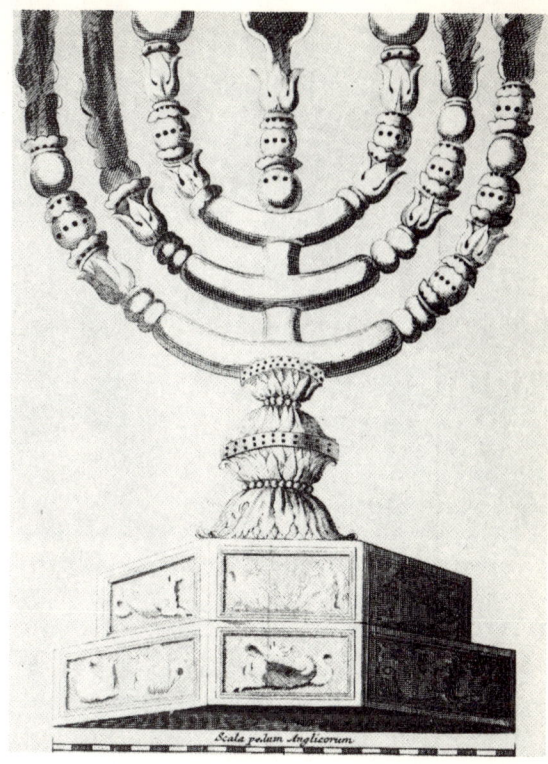

A picture of the seven branched Temple menorah. It was in a menorah such as this that the miracle of the holy oil was said to have occurred.

Later on, when people asked why the holiday of Chanukah should be celebrated for eight days, someone told the following story: In order to make the Temple holy again, the eternal light *(Ner Tamid)* had to be lit once again, but it required specially prepared oil. The Jewish soldiers searched the Temple, but there was only one small flask of pure holy oil to be found, so thoroughly had the place been looted by the Syrians. This was just enough to keep the light burning for one night. The next day, however, the light was still burning. And while the priests were busy preparing a new supply of oil, the light burned on for eight days! This was the reason, people said, that it was decided to observe the holiday for eight days.

It is not really important why Judah called for an eight-day celebration. Perhaps it was

A Syrian war elephant.

A modern day reenactment of the Chanukah story.

to take the place of Sukkot, the observance of which had been missed in the war year. What is important to know is that Chanukah is a holiday that recalls the *dedication* of the Temple to Jewish worship. The Jews had had to fight for this right. In Judah's time it meant the right to remove the Greek statues and idols and other things, impure from the religious viewpoint, out of the Temple.

The act of Chanukah, of dedication, is what gave the festival of Chanukah its importance, for it celebrated the first war fought for religious freedom. Ever since that time it has been a source of encouragement to all persecuted people of the world, giving them hope that with the help of God they also will one day be able to live and worship in their own way.

B. Growth of Chanukah Customs

One of the interesting things about Chanukah is that the *Bible* does not relate this story. It is found instead in the Books of the Maccabees, which were written by Jews but are not in the Bible. There were a number of more or less sacred books that Jews read and studied, but not all of them were selected by the rabbis to be included in the Bible. The books that were left out came in time to be called by a special name, the Apocrypha.

Some Jewish groups—the Falashas of Ethiopia, for instance—followed only what the Torah commanded. Since Chanukah is not mentioned there, they did not keep it in days gone by. When they came to Israel some years ago, they learned what Chanukah stands for and they, too, began to celebrate the holiday.

Nor was Chanukah kept by the Jews of India, the B'nei Israel. They had fled Palestine in the early days of the Greek-Syrian oppression, just before the time of Judah Maccabee.

The Books of the Maccabees do not lay down exact rules as to how Chanukah is to be observed; they simply say that Judah Maccabee ordered an eight-day celebration. The customs we follow today grew up in various countries from time to time, as our people celebrated Chanukah from year to year.

A beautifully ornamented nineteenth century Chanukah menorah made in Germany.

A very rare menorah of about the 9th century. The triangular trough for the shamash candle shows that this is a Chanukah menorah.

In ancient times there used to be a festival of lights in the Palestine area. Our ancestors also kindled these lights, but after 165 B.C.E. they lit them in honor of the victory of the Maccabees.

The holiday begins on the 25th of Kislev. Nowhere, however, was there a rule as to the way the lighting was to be done in honor of Chanukah, the new holiday.

So, even a hundred years after the first Chanukah, the discussion was still going on. Rabbi Shammai said that the festival must start with the lighting of eight lights on the first night, seven on the next, and so on, with only one lamp to be lit on the eighth night. But Rabbi Hillel, who lived at the same time, said that it should begin with one light on the first night, and increase each night, until on the final night eight lamps (or candles) should shine in all their brightness.

We know who won!

The procedure for the lighting of the candles in the Chanukah *menorah* (candelabrum) came about, as you can see, through the decision of the people. They liked Hillel's method, and in time Shammai's ideas were practically forgotten. Other customs became atttached to Chanukah in the same way. That is, the people did whatever would make the holiday gay and enjoyable. It was a time to be happy, remembering the wonderful events of those days.

Just think! The Jews were small in number, with no standing army, without chariots or elephants or stacks of weapons; yet they defeated the mighty Syrian-Greek army! And for what did they fight? To take slaves? To conquer land? To build themselves a new reputation among their neighbors? Not at all! All they wanted was the right to study the Torah, to worship in their beloved Jewish way, and to follow Jewish customs that made their lives pleasant and meaningful.

The Maccabee victory had made all this possible, and so the Jews lit candles every night in their honor, both in the synagogue and at home. By the time our great-grandfathers were children in Eastern Europe, the custom of using Chanukah week for festive meals and parties had developed. Every family served *latkes* (potato pancakes) at least once, and tried to provide a goose or other special dish or delicacy during the week.

Chanukah comes in the winter; families spend much time indoors. They therefore had to provide gay things to do at home in honor of the holiday. For the children, there was the game of *draydl* (spinning top in English, *svivon* in Hebrew). The draydl had a Hebrew letter on each of its four sides: *Nun, Gimel, Hay, Shin*. These are the first letters of a Hebrew sentence (*Nes Gadol Haya Sham*), which means, "A great miracle happened there."

They not only spun the top, but used it for betting in family or friendly games. Everyone put something into the pot at the start: beans, nuts, pennies, or whatever. If the *Nun* came up the player didn't put in or take out anything. He simply gave up his turn. If the *Shin* showed, he had to put another bean or nut

43

A Chanukah celebration in Germany in the nineteenth century by the famous German painter, Moritz Oppenheim.

into the pot; if he got a *Hay,* he won half of the pot; if he was really lucky, the *Gimel* turned up and he won the whole pot, and then they started all over again.

The grown-ups very often started playing cards. Some people say this Chanukah custom grew out of a situation that developed in the time of the Syrian oppression, when Jews were forbidden to gather together to study Torah or follow Jewish observances. They came together to study anyway, but took with them cards or other games, and when Syrian soldiers or police approached they quickly hid their religious books and began spinning the tops or playing the card games.

Children loved all these Chanukah customs, especially receiving Chanukah *gelt* (money). Most Jews of Eastern Europe were poor, so there were few occasions when children would get gifts or money. But Chanukah was something special, so even the poorest parents would bring out a few coins to give their children, which they could then spend as they pleased. But poor and rich alike could certainly share equally in one aspect of the holiday: they could all feel happy about the great victory of the Maccabees. They could all sing the great songs that were written for Chanukah: the *Maoz Tsur, Hanerot Hallalu, Mi Y'mallel, Chanukah Oy Chanukah,* and a host of others. They could all retell the stories and legends of the festival, and perform little plays about it, and they could all dance gaily—out of the sheer joy of Chanukah.

C. Chanukah in the United States Today

Because the Bible does not mention Chanukah, and it is not one of the holidays commanded by God, some Jews in the past considered it a minor festival. It had no special service in the synagogue, and it was not a holiday to be observed by resting; so it did not appear to require significant religious observance. In modern times, however, and especially in the United States, it came to be one of the most widely celebrated holidays in the Hebrew year.

Giving Chanukah Gelt.

Chanukah gifts.

One of the reasons is that Chanukah is a very democratic holiday. Here in America we give honor to the Pilgrims for leaving Europe in order to worship as they wished. And the first amendment to our Constitution separated church and State so that the government would not be able to favor any one religion over another. American Jews may well be proud that our ancestors were the first to fight for the establishment of the right of a people to their own religion and way of life.

Our people kept Chanukah alive, also, because it gave them encouragement when they were persecuted or discriminated against. It always held hope that a time would come when Jews would be free and equal everywhere.

Another reason for making Chanukah an important holiday in America is that it comes near Christmas time. In the public schools our children are taught Christmas carols every December. Radio and television are full of Christmas songs and stories. Wherever one goes today, as in years past, for weeks before Christmas the stores and shops are full of its symbols. This is a holiday that Jews can not freely participate in, for it celebrates the birth of what Christians call the Messiah, the "Son of God and Savior of mankind." It is a religious belief that is foreign to Judaism, and although Jesus is called the Prince of Peace, his "followers" brought death and terror to many Jewish communities for more than 1,500 years.

To counteract the Christmas atmosphere, Jewish parents began to emphasize Chanukah at home so that their children would not feel left out of all the gaiety and excitement of the season. The Jewish religious and Sunday schools did the same, and soon many Jewish families began to rediscover the beauty and meaning of Chanukah and to enjoy its celebration.

Some rather interesting things happened in America simply because Chanukah and Christmas come at about the same time. Instead of giving Chanukah gelt, many Jewish parents began to give presents, just as their Christian neighbors did. And since it is customary in our country for Christians to wrap Christmas presents in colorful paper, Jews began to produce special holiday wrapping paper, with all kinds of gay Chanukah symbols on them. Some families made it a custom to give a small gift each night of the festival, others contented themselves with giving presents on the first and fifth and eighth days. There is no rule about this; individual families decide for themselves how they wish to arrange the giving of Chanukah gelt or gifts.

In many families a Chanukah party is held for the children and their Jewish and Chris-

A group of American soldiers conduct Chanukah services around a huge electric menorah at Fort Jackson, North Carolina.

tian friends. Latkes are usually served, there is an exchange of gifts or a grab bag, and the children play draydl. The homes are gaily decorated, the Chanukah lights are lit, the children sing the songs of the holiday and often listen to phonograph records about Chanukah.

In the religious schools there are many more things to do for Chanukah. There are class parties. The children learn special songs and poems, make holiday decorations for the classroom and home, attend gala school assemblies and stage Chanukah plays. Of course, they learn about the deeper, more serious meanings of Chanukah too, but all human beings, and children particularly, enjoy it when fun and gaiety go along with the seriousness.

D. Modern Israel Celebrates Chanukah

Modern Israel also delights in Chanukah, but not because it is close to Christmas. Actually, one hears very little about Christmas in Israel, since there are so few Christians there. In Israel, Chanukah is significant because it stands for the victory of a small nation over its powerful enemy. Israel is surrounded by unfriendly Arab countries that are continually building up their armies and very openly declaring their intention of destroying Israel! Chanukah is a reminder to the Israelis that the Jews overcame such difficulties before.

Modern Israel, whose people fought fiercely and bravely in 1948 in order to establish a Jewish homeland on the soil where our Biblical ancestors lived, has made Chanukah a national holiday. The schools are closed and many families take vacation trips throughout the country.

The emphasis in the Israeli celebration is upon glorifying the Maccabee victory in the war against Antiochus, much as in early days of our own country we glorified the victory of George Washington's small army over the might of Great Britain.

A Bukharian family dressed in their traditional clothes light the menorah.

A group of runners in the torch-bearing relay race.

But it is also a time for latkes (*l'vivot* in Hebrew) and for playing the draydl. If you were playing with an Israeli draydl, however, your draydl would have the letter *Peh* instead of the *Shin*. Can you guess why? It's because in Israel alone they can say "A great miracle happened *here*." (The Hebrew word for here is *Poh*.)

It is mainly a holiday of Israeli youth, upon whom the future of Israel depends. Every year young men of the Maccabee Sports Club hold a torch-bearing relay race. The first runner begins from Modi'in, the town in which Mattathias began the fight against the Syrian tyrant Antiochus. After a ceremony at what are believed to be the graves of the five Maccabean brothers, a torch is lighted and handed to the lead runner.

He runs with it to the next town, hands it to another runner, who carries it to another town, and so on through thirty-eight towns and villages. At the nineteenth annual relay in 5724 (1964), the runners stopped at the site of the ancient fortress of Masada. Here a leading archaeologist accepted it on behalf of his society, which had dug up many important relics there.

That year the torch went from runner to young runner. When it came to Tel Aviv, it was handed by Israel's top long-distance runner, Jair Pantilat, to Chief Rabbi Yehuda Unterman. It then was run to *Yad* Chaim Weizmann, the memorial place of Israel's first President, where it was taken by his widow, Mrs. Vera Weizmann, and used in kindling the Chanukah lights there.

The cross-country run ended with the handing of the torch to President Zalman Shazar at his residence in Jerusalem. President Shazar then used the torch to light the Chanukah candles atop the capitol.

The memory of Chanukah is kept alive the year around in the name of Israel's greatest

The start of the torch-bearing relay race in Israel. The torch of freedom passes from hand to hand.

A group of hardy hikers on a Chanukah trek to the mountain fortress of Masada.

Memorial inscription of the 10th Roman Legion, which was stationed at Jerusalem.

sports club, the Maccabeans, whose soccer team has already achieved great note in other countries as well. They meet and practice athletics in a large underground hall. On Chanukah they have a special celebration, decorating the hall and holding a great *neshef* (eve-

Masada, this fortress high on a rock near the Dead Sea, was the last Jewish stronghold to fall to the Roman conquerors following the destruction of the Temple.
Today, in Israel army recruits march to the top of the mountain. There, they pledge (see Hebrew sign) "Masada will not fall again."

ning festivity), sometimes in the form of a masquerade ball.

Young people of strength and courage take walking trips at Chanukah time through the desert, to visit ancient fortresses and places where Judah Maccabee and his followers fought the good fight for freedom of religion. These pilgrimages are not pleasant little hikes! There are difficult hills to be climbed and it is often hard to find a safe path among

A giant electric menorah lights the skies of Israel for miles around.

The electric Menorah atop the Great Synagogue in Tel Aviv.

An Eastern European 19th-century draydl made of wood.

the rocks. And in the desert there is always the danger of thirst and sandstorm.

In the streets of Israel's cities there are torchlight processions, with children bearing lighted candles, lamps or torches, and singing loudly the songs of the holiday and of their schools. There are parties and celebrations everywhere.

In all of Israel no house is so poor that the

The spoils of the Second Temple carried in the triumphal procession of Titus, who conquered Jerusalem in 70 C.E. Shown here is an 18th-century Italian copy in bronze based on the Arch of Titus in Rome.

lights of Chanukah cannot shine in their windows. A family may not own a fancy *Chanukiyah* (Chanukah menorah), but they can fashion one out of saucers of oil (the ancient form of lamp), or out of egg-cups or clay. What is important for Israel is the memory of the deeds of the people under the leadership of the Maccabees.

A seven branched Menorah is, in fact, the symbol of the modern State of Israel. It appears on the coins and on the stamps of the country. The government even issues special coins to be given as Chanukah *kesef* (money) for the children! And these, of course, bear the menorah on one side.

Just as the Statue of Liberty greets all who enter New York harbor, a huge menorah stands on the roof of the Great Synagogue in Tel Aviv, lighting up the whole city for all the eight days and nights of Chanukah.

Many other towns have these great menorahs; in Jerusalem a menorah glows in front of the Jewish Agency building, and another on the Bezalel Art School roof. They are also placed atop the high watertowers.

The Arch of Titus in Rome was erected to commemorate the Roman victory over the Jews in 70 C.E.

This Jewish menorah, with its branches that spread out like triumphant and gracious arms, sheds a light that is recognized throughout the world, the light of freedom and faith in God. The great Roman Empire that once conquered the Jews of ancient Judea, that destroyed their government and state and tried to destroy their religion as well, has itself disappeared from living history. But the Jews live on as Jews in their own sovereign State on their ancient soil.

One of the things the ancient Romans left behind is the Arch of Titus, in Rome, which they put up in honor of their military victory over the Jews in 70 C.E. On this arch they depicted the Jews leaving Jerusalem as captives headed for slavery. Some of the Jews are shown carrying a menorah.

Whenever the Jews were forced to leave a country, or when they decided to go of their own accord, they always took with them some kind of menorah—either the seven-branched one for the Sabbath or the nine-branched one for Chanukah, sometimes both. The Chanukiyah is a living symbol out of our past. From it comes a living light, a light that stands for freedom of religion.

HEBREW HOLIDAY TERMS

CHANUKAH

Chanukah	חֲנֻכָּה	dedication
menorah	מְנוֹרָה	a lamp
s'vivon	סְבִיבוֹן	a spinning top (draydl in Yiddish)
l'vivot	לְבִיבוֹת	pancakes (latkes in Yiddish)
Kislev	כִּסְלֵו	ninth month

TU BISH'VAT

A. A No-History Holiday

In the solemn parade of great religious and historical festivals, the holiday of *Tu Bish'vat* may seem to be a thin little affair, without much importance. After all, it commemorates no great event in history, no person of any significance is connected with it, and there is no special service or prayer set aside for it in the synagogue. And yet Tu Bish'vat has stood the test of time, for it has been kept alive by our people since its start in ancient times as an agricultural festival.

This is easier to understand when you give it its real name, the "New Year of the Trees," the name that really describes it. Then you can see Tu Bish'vat for what it really is—a lovely, lively springtime holiday, full of meaning for people who are interested in every growing thing, and that, of course, means children also.

Although trees are the heroes of the holiday, we still call it by the Hebrew date on which it falls: *Tu* (standing for the letters *tet* and *vav*, which together add up to fifteen);

Trees play an important part in the growth of the modern State of Israel. Young Israelis bring their saplings for planting.

Carefully the youngsters cover the fragile shoots of the saplings. In years to come the wastelands of Israel will burst into foliage with millions of green budding trees.

Bish'vat (meaning "in the month of Sh'vat"). There was a time when people said *Chamishah Asar* (which is the way one says "fifteen" in Hebrew), but the Israelis have popularized the shorter way of expressing it.

In Israel, the month of Sh'vat comes at a time of changing weather. Its beginning is chilly, for it is still part of the rainy season, but by the middle of the month the heavy rains have usually come to an end. Almost suddenly the flowers and trees burst into bloom. The fragrance and loveliness of springtime soon cover the land. This is the time when new trees are planted in Israel. On Tu Bish'vat the Jewish National Fund, which has planted millions of trees in the former wastelands of Israel, organizes a great tree-planting expedition in practically every part of the country.

Even before the founding of the State of Israel, Tu Bish'vat had already become a children's festival. One year, near Tel-Aviv, hundreds of school children marched into a green field, each wearing a wreath of green leaves, while a band played music and the blue and white flag flew gaily in the spring breeze. The children sang and danced, and then all of them, carrying spades, hoes and watering cans, marched up to receive from their teachers the tiny saplings to be planted. Then they spread out over the field in groups of three; while one child dug with the spade, another child fetched water, and a third carefully set the new little tree into place in the soil, patting the earth firmly down around it so that it would stand straight and grow tall.

Tu Bish'vat is eagerly looked forward to by the children in every village and town. The homes are decorated with flowers and green leaves. The children put on white shirts or blouses and they all march singing onto the village green to plant new trees around the flagpole, under the flag of Zion. Then they go

A tree farm in Israel.

Pruning young trees at a tree farm in Israel.

planting flowers and trees in various places and gardens in the area. It is a happy, exciting day.

B. The Meaning of Tu Bish'vat Today

In other countries, too, Jews observe the New Year of the Trees. In India they have special parties, where all kinds of fruits and nuts and different colored wines are served. The schools prepare parties for the children, and gifts of fruit are sent to families which cannot afford to buy them.

Since the seasons in various countries differ from those of Israel, it is not possible to observe Tu Bish'vat in the same way in every land.

In the United States, for instance, Jews who live in New York, or in other parts of the northern half of the country, could hardly plant trees in honor of the day, since Tu Bish'vat time comes usually in the dead of winter. In many classrooms, however, the teachers prepare special celebrations during which something that can grow indoors is planted in a pot or window box. The school will also provide *bokser,* the fruit of the carob tree, which is also called by some "St. John's Bread." Carob trees are plentiful in Israel, and large amounts of bokser are shipped to the United States for Tu Bish'vat observances. Another custom of the day which is kept up by the Jewish schools is that of eating whatever Israeli fruits are available at the time.

The custom that has taken hold most firmly in the United States and elsewhere in recent times is the buying of tree certificates from the Jewish National Fund, which arranges to have a tree planted in whatever forest the buyer requests for each certificate paid for. There are many fully planted forests in Israel that were paid for by contributions made at Tu Bish'vat time. The idea of help-

A young Israeli picks carobs (bokser) for a Tu Bish'vat party.

ing to replenish the forests of Israel, which were destroyed during ancient wars and which fell away during centuries of neglect, has taken hold among the Jews to such an extent that people often buy tree certificates all through the year. They do this to honor a birth, a graduation, *bar mitzvah* or anniversary, or as a way of remembering the passing of a loved one.

The Jewish chaplain and a master sergeant at the Marine Corps Depot at Parris Island, South Carolina, plant a tree on Tu Bish'vat in memory of their comrades-in-arms.

And if you ask why trees mean so much to our people, the answer is that it isn't just trees but *trees for Israel*. Trees mean shade and wood for our Israeli cousins; they provide, through forests, a place of recreation, an area for animals to live in, and a strengthening of the soil, which can then withstand heavy rains. Rows and stands of trees provide windbreaks that help protect fields and orchards. In short, planting trees in Israel is a way of helping the country to grow and flourish, and it is good that there is a Tu Bish'vat to act as an annual reminder of the need.

But even before there was a Jewish State in Palestine, the Jews of Europe, practically housebound because of winter at Tu Bish'vat time, nevertheless thought of trees and flowers and fruits as the holiday approached, for they knew it was springtime in the land of the Bible, their ancient homeland. There God's good earth was ready to turn green. Jews honored the workings of the universe; in their mind it was the hand of God at work, and so, even without a synagogue service, they set aside time to keep Tu Bish'vat, as we continue to do now.

HEBREW HOLIDAY TERMS

TU BISH'VAT

Tu Bish'vat	ט״ו בִּשְׁבָט	15th day in month of Sh'vat
Rosh Hashanah La-ilanot	רֹאשׁ הַשָּׁנָה לָאִילָנוֹת	start of the year for the trees
charuv	חָרוּב	carob tree (bokser in Yiddish)
Sh'vat	שְׁבָט	eleventh month

PURIM

A. A Bible Story to Explain a Holiday

As you have learned, there is a very real, full and historic story behind Chanukah, although the books that give the details of it are not part of the Bible. The story behind our next holiday, *Purim,* is in the Bible. In fact, a whole book, even though a short one, is devoted to it. Although in this entire "Book of Esther" the name of God is not mentioned, and God does not command the Jews to observe the holiday of Purim, yet our people have been observing the 14th of Adar for over two thousand years.

Let us see how *Megillat Esther* (the Book of Esther) explains the origin of the holiday.

The ancient Jews were once part of the Persian Empire (Persia is now called Iran). A large number of Jews preferred to remain in Persia even after Emperor Cyrus told them they might return to Palestine. Many did go back, but many others went on living in peace in the city of Shushan, the capital of Persia.

There came a time when the whole empire was ruled by a king named Ahasuerus.

As the Bible tells the story, this king did

Illustrated Persian manuscript in Hebrew letters. The Persians ruled over Babylonia during the time of the Amoraim, and many Jews lived in all parts of the Persian empire.

The tomb of King Cyrus.

not know or care very much about what was going on in his country. He was interested mostly in feasting and enjoying himself, so he left much of the empire's affairs in the hands of his minister-in-chief, Haman. It is even possible that he might never have bothered with the Jews of Shushan if he had not become angry with his queen Vashti and sent her away.

His advisers then arranged for a country-wide search for the fairest girl in the land to be his new queen. Many young women were brought to the palace, and the fairest one was Esther, a Jewess. On the advice of her older cousin, Mordecai, she did not tell King Ahasuerus that she was Jewish, and apparently he never asked.

Mordecai spent much time around the palace watching over his young cousin, and on one occasion he happened to overhear two guards plotting to kill the king. Mordecai sent word to King Ahasuerus about it and the two conspirators were caught and put to death. This, of course, put him in favor with the king, but it happened at just the wrong time for Haman. For Haman had meanwhile grown to hate Mordecai intensely. Haman had given orders that everybody at the palace was to bow down before him as he passed, but Mordecai alone refused to do so. Whenever Haman went by, the sight of Mordecai standing up while all others kneeled threw him into a fury.

Haman found out that Mordecai was a Jew, and he decided to get rid of all the Jews in Persia. Catching the king in the right mood one day, he told him a made-up story about a strange and foreign people in Persia who he said did not obey the Persian law. This was not a good thing for the country, he told the king, and he suggested that Ahasuerus give him authority to slay these people. The king

Xerxes I, King of Persia (485-465 B.C.E.) from a relief at Persepolis. According to the opinion of many scholars, he is the king referred to as Ahasuerus in the Book of Esther.

In a 17th-century *Purimshpiel* sketch, downcast Haman leads triumphant Mordecai. Note the costumes: they belong to the period when the play was presented, not to the ancient Persia in which the story is set.

Persian soldiers.

King Ahasuerus and his merrymaking courtiers from a seventeeth century Polish Megillah.

did not know what people Haman was talking about, but he didn't care. What impressed the king was that Haman felt so strongly about it that he offered to pay a large sum into the treasury in order to get rid of the "problem" people. The king must have assumed therefore that Haman was right. He gave Haman his ring with the seal of the state on it, which empowered him to give any orders he wished, and to give them in the name of the king.

Now, thought Haman, gleefully, he could take his revenge on Mordecai! He cast lots (the ancient word for this was Purim) to set a day for the slaughter of the Hebrews in Persia. The day chosen was the 13th of the Hebrew month Adar. Haman then sent special letters to his military commanders to carry out the attack on the Jews on that day. But Mordecai's fate was to be left to Haman himself. For Mordecai, Haman built a special gallows upon which he planned to hang his enemy.

Mordecai, when he learned of Haman's plot, went to Esther to plead with her to tell the king of Haman's wicked scheme. But Esther was afraid. In those days, no one, not even the queen, had the right to come into the presence of the king unless sent for. If anyone came unbidden, and the king became irritated, he or she could be killed on the

A wall painting from the Dura Europos Synagogue. Haman leads Mordecai's horse and King Ahasuerus and Queen Esther are sitting on their thrones.
Yale University Art Gallery

spot. But Mordecai explained to Esther that the lives of her people depended on her alone. She must go at once to the king.

So Esther took the risk. She stood before the king, nearly fainting with fear, while the guard raised his sword, ready to slay her if the king commanded it. But the king's heart was touched when he saw who it was, and he gave the sign for her to approach unharmed.

Esther invited the king to a banquet, and he accepted. She also invited Haman. At the party she told the king about the evil plot Haman had worked out to slaughter the Jews. She explained that she, too, was a Jewess and would be killed. The king was furious. So Haman had tricked him into this mess! The king ordered Haman hung on the very gallows he had built for Mordecai!

This was not the end of the story, however. In those days in Persia, once a written order went out in the name of the king it could not be changed. Therefore, Haman's agents would still follow their orders to attack the Jews. The king therefore gave Mordecai per-

mission to give weapons to the Jews, and to make it known that the Jews would be allowed to defend themselves. The Book of Esther tells us that in some places the Jews were attacked, but they fought valiantly and survived. The king appointed Mordecai as his chief minister in place of Haman, and

Traditonal tomb of Esther and Mordecai in Hamadan, Iran. (Persia).

Purim is a time for merrymaking, with masks, greggers, hamantashen and Megillah reading.

honored Esther, his Jewish queen, above all other women.

And the 14th day of Adar—the day after the attack—was made a holiday!

B. Some Special Purims

The name Haman has come to stand for every oppressor of Israel, Mordecai for every wise leader of the Jews in their time of trouble, and Esther for every Jewish heroine.

Purim, in fact, signifies a festival of deliverance of Jews from any threatened evil. Communities and even families used to keep individual Purims every year, like birthdays. The Jews of Egypt, for instance, had a special Purim in memory of an event in the year 1524 C. E. A governor of that country had threatened to massacre its Jews because they would not join him in a revolt against the Sultan of Turkey, who ruled Egypt. The governor had already imprisoned many Jews, when a revolt took place against *him* and *he* was slain. The Jews as a result were saved. A book was written to tell the story, and on their special Purim this book was read in the Egyptian synagogues.

The Jews of Frankfurt in Germany also celebrated a special Purim, this one for being saved from an attack on their ghetto in 1614. And in 1804 a rabbi of Vilna, who survived a gunpowder explosion which wrecked his and other homes, decreed a family fast and a special Purim festival each year on that date. Other special Purims were kept in Tiberias, Israel; in Saragossa, Spain; in Narbonne, France; in Prague, Czechoslovakia; in Rhodes, Greece, and in other cities.

C. Purim in Eastern Europe

For Jews who kept very close to tradition, and these were in the majority in Eastern Europe, Purim began on the Sabbath before the 14th of Adar. Many Jews believed that Mordecai was a descendant of King Saul, and that Haman was a descendant of Israel's an-

In the fourteenth century the Jews of Syracuse, Sicily, were saved from persecution. The above Megillah from Syracuse was written to commemorate this deliverance.

ויהי בימי המלך שאראגושאנוש מלך אדיר וחזק היה והיו רד"ת
ממשלתו כחמשת אלפי איש מבני ישראל כלם חכמים ונבונים
ראשי אלפי ישראל המה לבד מבחוריהם ונעריהם ונשיהם ובניהם
וטפם שתים עשרה קהלות קדושות בנים באבני גזית ועמוד
שיש כלילות יופי ממולאים בתר"שי"ש וכה מנהג ומשפט היהוד"ן
האלה בעבר המלך דרך שוק היהודים היו מוציאים שלשה ספרי
תורה מכל קהלה שלשים ושש ספרים מעוטפים בבגדי רקמ"ה
ובתיקי כסף וזהב ורמונים ותפוחי כסף וזהב במשכיורת כסף
בראשי ספרים ומברכים למלך בקול גדול ורם וכל העם עונים
אחריהם אמן ויהי היום נקהלו שנים עשר וחמי ישראל וארבעה
ועשרים דייניהם לאמר לא טוב אנחנו עושים לצאת עם תורת
אלהינו חיים ומלך עולם לפני עובד אלילים ופסילים נוערי
נסדו יחדיו להכין שלשה תיקין ריקים מכל קהלה וקהלה מעוטפים

64

cient enemy, Amalek. So they added on the Sabbath before Purim, as the reading for the *Maftir,* the three verses in Deuteronomy 25 referring to Amalek's attack on the weary Israelites after the Exodus from Egypt—"Remember what Amalek did unto thee by the way as ye came forth out of Egypt . . ." They also selected for the reading of the *Haftarah* that part of the Book of Samuel which tells of Saul's war against Agag, King of the Amalekites.

Strict observers of Talmudic laws also fast on the day before Purim, because Queen Esther fasted on the day before she went in to see the king. But it was only a few, actually, who kept *Taanit Esther* (the Fast of Esther). Everybody else in the East European *shtetl* (small town) was busy getting ready for the festivities. In every oven, three-cornered cakes filled with poppyseed were being baked. These were popularly called *hamantashen* ("Haman's pockets" in Yiddish). Women also prepared three-cornered dough patties filled with meat (*kreplach*) to put into the soup.

An eighteenth century Russian case for containing a scroll of Esther.

A form for baking hamantashen; Poland, 19th century.

An ingenious wooden *gregger* made in Poland in 1935, depicts Haman and his 20th-century counterpart, Hitler.

In the synagogue there was an air of excitement and celebration, not of solemnity. Contributions of coins were made in memory of the ancient tax for the Temple. And as the Book of Esther was read, everybody, the younger people especially, listened eagerly for every mention of the name of Haman, which they then tried to drown out with their *greggers* (noisemakers). And as if that was not enough, they also stamped their feet to express contempt more resoundingly.

The Purim service seems designed mainly for the reading of the *Megillah* (the scroll of Esther). It certainly was not a solemn occasion, such as the Sabbath and other holiday services. Shops remained open and people did their work as usual. But there was holiday in the air; hamantashen were eaten, beggars came to every house and were given money or food, and messengers were kept running all over town carrying *shalach manot* (presents) from relatives and friends. Sugar candies were a special Purim treat, often made in the form of animals, toys, little figures of Mordecai on horseback, or whatever the clever housewife could think up.

The real excitement of the day was the *Purimshpiel* (the Purim show) put on by the Purim players. These were generally pious Jews who took up acting just for this day. Men played all the parts, even that of Queen Esther! They wore paper crowns, red cardboard noses or paper cheeks, and flaxen curls pasted on their heads. At the height of the day's festivities they would comically act out the parts of Haman, Mordecai, Esther and King Ahasuerus, in a way to make everyone laugh.

Purim players in a copper engraving of 1657. Their weapons are brooms and mops!

A seventeenth century illuminated French Megillah.

The Purim play usually had many actors, but not every Jew in town could be in it. Everybody had fun in his own way, however. Some bounced down the street turning somersaults, others danced crazily, whirled around banging drums and cymbals, or blew horns, while still others whistled, sang and shouted. Purim shpielers, alone or in groups, went from house to house singing songs, doing a little dance, acting a little skit; anything at all to make people laugh and to get in return coins or goodies or something to drink.

It was like the Mardi Gras carnival that the French brought with them when they settled in New Orleans, Louisiana, some two hundred years ago. It is still a famous event in that city, and it is interesting that Mardi Gras takes place around Purim time. Both celebrations occur when winter is coming to an end, and people are in a mood for gaiety.

That's the way Jews of Eastern Europe felt at Purim for hundreds of years. And even though Jews in the past were generally not heavy drinkers, they did drink more at Purim time. In fact, it was considered a *mitzvah* (a holy commandment) to get tipsy on Purim! Not to become disorderly or harmful, of course, but even the rabbis said that it was all right to drink *"ad lo yada"* (until one didn't know) the difference between "blessed be Mordecai" and "cursed be Haman." What was important was to have fun on Purim and enjoy the day. Modern Israelis decided to make one word out of the three little Hebrew words—*adloyada*—when they looked for a Hebrew word for the "carnival" that became a Purim custom.

By the way, some people say that "13" is considered unlucky because the 13th of Adar was chosen as the day for Haman's attack on the Jews.

D. Purim in Israel

Purim is, in a sense, the celebration of the continued survival of Judaism throughout

67

Jonah can't seem to escape from the whale in this float in a Tel Aviv Adloyada procession.

the ages. It is therefore natural that it should be one of the prime holidays of modern Israel. The State is itself the living evidence of Jewish survival, not only of the religion of Judaism, but also of the Jewish people as a nation.

Thus, at Purim, every town in the State of Israel becomes a stage. There are masquerades and balls and parties everywhere, and processions with bands and floats. Dances, concerts and plays take over the country.

There's no school, of course, and no traffic in the streets—no business traffic, that is; for the streets of Israel on that day belong to the Jewish citizens. In Israel, naturally, Jews are not restricted to their own little section of town as they were in Eastern Europe. In Israel the whole country, practically, is Jewish, and the children throng the streets with their masks and their noise-makers and their fancy costumes.

Everywhere there is a carnival mood. Even the police lose their seriousness and sometimes join in the dancing. If they try to control anybody who's too wild, the answer is likely to be, "What are you making a fuss about? Don't you know it's Purim? Come and join us!"

Restaurants and cafes are crowded with visitors and residents. Sidewalks, roofs, balconies are packed with people waiting to see the processions and the "mummers" (masquerade performers) presenting the story of Purim in all kinds of ways, from the serious and inspirational to the absurdly comical.

In Tel Aviv, a great procession begins in the cool of the evening, about five o'clock. Headed by mounted police, trucks come bearing elaborate floats of all the chief characters in the story of Esther—the lovely young queen with her attendant maidens, Mordecai riding his horse, the villain Haman with his ten sons, and all the rest.

It is considered quite proper for commercial floats to take part: men dress up to advertise food or wine products of Israeli firms, for example. A prize is awarded for the best float, which might be won by a school or an institution or a business firm. Once, when a Yemenite girl was chosen as Queen Esther, the Yemenite community came out gaily dressed in their national costumes, singing and dancing in their wonderful way, to express their joy and pride.

In Jerusalem, which is less industrial and more a city of students and professionals, the mood is quieter, but it is even more interesting to visitors; for Jews who have settled there

A float in the Adloyada parade.

from varied communities celebrate, each group according to its own tradition.

The Iranian (Persian) Jews eat their meal seated on the beautiful woven carpets for which Iran has always been famous. The father, with his long dark beard, wears a turban of cloth and a belted white gown striped with silver. (In Iran the Jews had to keep Purim at home, as it was forbidden in olden times for Jews to go outdoors in holiday clothing.)

The Yemenite Jews also sit around on a carpet, chanting oriental songs, while the father smokes his long water-pipe. Their *seudah* (festival meal) is made of fresh, sweet dishes, instead of their usual highly spiced food. The young girls wear silver rings, and they gaily dance, shaking their tambourines.

The father of the Kurdish-Jewish family stands at his door to welcome his guests. For Purim he puts on a modern jacket over the wide, bloomer-like trousers. Where are the children? They are all out in the streets playing Purim games, if the weather permits, for Jerusalem is often cold and rainy at this time of year.

Jews from the Caucasus keep Purim by wearing their native robes with knives at their belts, exhibiting their old-time folk-dances, squatting and kicking out their legs, throwing their knives and dancing around them.

In the kibbutzim (collective settlements) throughout Israel there is a great spirit of gaiety—music, dances, theatrical performances with real stage settings, masques and shows and beauty-queens, mock circuses, games and fun and contests.

The joy of survival reigns supreme!

E. Celebrating Purim in the United States

In the United States and other Western nations today, there is also a joyous spirit at Purim, but it is usually not celebrated with outdoor processions and parades. Synagogues and Jewish schools have Megillah readings where the children drown out the mention of Haman with greggers and other noise-makers. The Jewish schools prepare adloyadas with all sorts of games. The children dress up in costumes and many children have Purim parties at home. The Jewish schools hold special assemblies to present Purimshpiels, and to sing the many lovely songs of Purim in Hebrew, Yiddish and English. In many of the homes as well as in the schools the children are served hamantashen.

Since Jews have always believed in sharing their joy and abundance with other Jews, it is still a custom with many American Jews to give shalach manot to friends and neighbors. In many American towns and cities Jews make a special effort to give to the needy of all races and religions at Purim time, in addition to the usual charities.

Some Purim customs of olden times are no longer to be seen today, neither in Europe nor in the United States. It was a custom in oriental (eastern) countries, for instance, for Jews to burn or hang images of Haman, which they made of wax or straw. It is likely that in more modern times they felt that this

A Purim play at Sunday School.

was too barbaric. There was also the fear among European Jews that Christians might misunderstand and think that the Jews meant these images to represent Jesus. Jews did not want their neighbors to think they were insulting the Christian faith. This was the reason, some writers say, why Jews living in Christian lands gave up this custom a long time ago.

What is remarkable about Purim is not that some of its customs have disappeared, but rather that so many of them have continued on to our own day. This has happened in spite of the fact that Purim is not one of the holidays commanded by Moses in the desert. It is in the Bible, but not in the Torah, yet it has lasted all these thousands of years. Some say it will never go out of fashion, because it is a reminder of all the narrow escapes that the Jewish people have had in their long history.

"Purim will be celebrated always." A twentieth century American youngster reads the ancient story from an illuminated Megillah scroll.

It seems to say that somehow the Jews will pull through. Our rabbis said a long time ago, "Though all other festivals may disappear, Purim will be celebrated for always."

HEBREW HOLIDAY TERMS

PURIM

Purim	פּוּרִים	lots (Haman chose the day for attacking Jews by casting lots)
Adar	אֲדָר	twelfth month
Megillah	מְגִלָּה	a scroll (book of the Bible)
Hadassah	הֲדַסָּה	Myrtle (Esther's Hebrew name)
ra-ashonim	רַעֲשָׁנִים	noisemakers (greggers in Yiddish)
mishlo-ach manot	מִשְׁלֹחַ מָנוֹת	sending portions
adloyada	עַדְלָיָדַע	until he would not know (Hebrew word for Purim Carnival)
Purim shpieler (Yiddish)	פּוּרִים שְׁפִּילֶער	Purim actor
hamantash (Yiddish)	הָמָנְטַאשׁ	Purim cake

PESACH

A. Passover and the Birth of the Jewish People

If you were asked, "Why can Passover (*Pesach*) be called the birthday of the people of Israel?" you would probably have to think a while before you could give an answer.

But what is a birthday, really? It is the anniversary of the day when a life begins. And when did the life of the Jews as a people begin?

For many centuries the Jews, who called themselves in ancient times the people of Israel, had been a group of wandering tribes, mostly shepherds; they were different from other tribes in one respect only, in that the Hebrews worshipped one God alone. But they were not yet a people with their own land and government. Certain events, however, brought the Hebrews to Egypt, where the first step was taken toward becoming a people.

It was Joseph, one of the twelve sons of Jacob, who brought the Hebrews down to Egypt. And for many years the Hebrews lived in peace in that country. Rulers came and went, without any disturbance to the descendants of the House of Jacob. But there came a time when a new Pharaoh ascended the Egyptian throne, a king "who knew not Joseph." This Pharaoh either had not heard of the great things Joseph had done for Egypt or else he didn't care. In any case, Pharaoh decided it was not safe to let a minority group live freely in Egypt. He enslaved the Hebrews, and they remained slaves for many generations. They lived in misery, feeling that God had abandoned them. They were surely far from thinking of themselves as a people in those days.

Then startling news came to them! A young prince by the name of Moses, brought up in the royal palace of the Pharaoh who now reigned, had come to visit their miser-

An ancient Egyptian wall-painting showing prisoners at work making bricks and building a wall.

able huts, and had not only shown much pity and kindness toward them, but had even declared himself to be a Jew like themselves. In fact, he had become so angry with an Egyptian overseer who was beating a Hebrew slave that Moses had killed the Egyptian. But the hope that might have sprung up in some hearts soon died, for Moses disappeared. He had fled into the desert to escape the Pharaoh's punishment.

After some years, however, Moses felt sure that he had been selected by God to bring His people out of Egypt into a land of freedom. He therefore returned to Egypt and with great courage faced the Pharaoh to demand that he set the Hebrews free. Pharaoh refused again and again, but finally, after Egypt suffered many plagues, the Egyptian ruler actually urged them to leave. The Hebrews set forth in a great hurry for fear the Pharaoh might change his mind. He did, as a matter of fact. He sent an army of chariots to pursue and recapture the Hebrews, but the fugitives were able to cross the Sea of Reeds (which people also call the Red Sea) on foot, while the heavy Egyptian chariots sank in its muddy waters.

Perhaps it was at that moment, when the Hebrews had crossed the Sea of Reeds in safety and saw Pharaoh's army going under, that some Hebrews could feel that they were a special people, with meaning and with a future. For it was surely a miracle! Only with

An Egyptian brick with the imprint of the seal of Rameses II.

The Egyptian rock temple of Abu Simbel. In front of the temple are four stone statues, each over sixty feet in height, of Rameses II.

the help of God could they have escaped the fearsome Egyptian army.

It was not a mere escape, Moses told his people. He saw in the Exodus from Egypt the hand of God, part of His design for the people of Israel. Moses led them to Mount Sinai, and bade them camp at the base of the Mount. Moses himself, amid lightning and thunder and much strangeness in the air, went to the top of Mount Sinai. When he returned to the people he assembled them together, and read to them the Torah and the Ten Command-

An Egyptian war-chariot, found painted on a tomb wall in Thebes, ancient capital of Egypt.

ments. And the people then said, *"Naase v'nishmah"* (We will do and we will obey).

In a sense, it was this that started them on the road to becoming a people. It was the acceptance of the Torah as their guide that bound all the tribes and families of Israel into one community, and made them the people of God. Afterwards, as they wandered forty years in the desert, with the Torah as their constitution, Moses organized a government for them. It was an altogether different kind of government for those days. In that ancient time of widespread tyranny, when kings had all the power and were even worshipped as gods, the people of Israel were organized into what could be called a republic. Not man, but only God, was their king. And there was a strong democratic spirit in the government that Moses set up, for it rested on the basic teaching of the Torah that all were equal.

Of course they were not equal in everything; some persons have more ability than others. There are men who can be teachers and judges; there are men who are able to explain and interpret the law of God and to enforce it. Some men have to be priests, to direct the religious ceremonials. But, while some individuals become different from others as a result of natural ability or superior education, this does not give them rights over others in the eyes of the law. All people, says the Torah, no matter what their work is, are commanded to act as good neighbors toward one another. No one was to consider himself better than anyone else, when it came to obeying the laws of the religion. Even kings were expected to observe the laws of the Torah, just like the ordinary citizens.

Pesach celebrates the escape from slavery in Egypt, but the vital result of the Exodus was the birth of the people of Israel as a nation. That is why we can say that Passover is the birthday of Israel, and we celebrate it by recounting its story every year on its anniversary, Nisan the 15th.

There is more to Passover than even the great event of the creating of a people bound together by a divine code of law.

It also celebrates the miraculous redeeming of Israel. While many of our festivals are occasions of thanking God for saving the Jews from oppression or destruction, this feast of Passover commemorates the most important redemption of all. Without it, there would have been no Torah, no Israel, and no Jewish people.

There is one more aspect of this holiday.

Passover comes in springtime, and has absorbed into itself an ancient nature-festival which the Hebrews observed from their earliest days. Almost from the beginning of human life on earth, people of the world must have been celebrating the coming of spring, each in a different way. Knowing nothing of the causes of the seasons, the earliest human beings were never quite sure that winter was not the death of the earth. So, when spring came again, their joy was intense, and they celebrated and made sacrifices.

So Passover is, first, Israel's "birthday," when their life as a people began; secondly, the festival of the freeing of the Jews from ancient captivity and oppression; thirdly, it is

Ancient Haggadah manuscript found in Cairo, Egypt.

the spring harvest festival, when the first grain harvest ripens and is cut.

B. Celebrating Passover in Temple Times

Passover became the most important holiday, the one on which the Jews felt the strongest desire to be all together, and to celebrate as one great family. Everyone in ancient times who could possibly do so came to Jerusalem for this purpose.

It was an obligation in ancient times for every Jerusalemite to consider his house open to other Jews coming to celebrate Passover. Everyone who came brought a goat or sheep for sacrifice, or perhaps only enough money to buy a pair of birds. So many came to the holy city that Jerusalem was usually crowded beyond imagination every Pesach. The main market place was jammed with visiting merchants from north, south, east and west, who spread out their wares: sheep and cattle for sacrifice, spices and herbs for the Passover *seder* (special Passover home service and meal), fabrics and ornaments for holiday clothes. Their tables and stands were covered with wheat cakes, fresh fish, wine and wine-syrups, olives, honey.

Since Passover is the celebration, and a symbolic repetition, of the events of the deliverance from Egypt, important changes were made in the daily life of the Jews during this holiday. Because the Jews left Egypt in great haste they had no time to prepare bread. Instead they baked the thin strips of unleavened dough in the hot sun. It is for this reason that we eat *matzah* (unleavened bread) during Passover. Not only must matzah be eaten, but every home had to be completely cleared of the slightest remains of *chametz* (leavened bread).

In ancient times, before the destruction of the Second Temple in 70 C.E., the sheep or goat which was used for the Passover sacrifice had to be completely eaten the first night of the holiday. Groups of people, sometimes every related family in a small village, would come together for the Pesach meal so as to be sure not to leave a single bit of the roasted meat for the morning.

Present-day Samaritans in Israel, who claim descent from the tribes of Ephraim and Manasseh, have their own customs. Here they bake matzot for Passover.

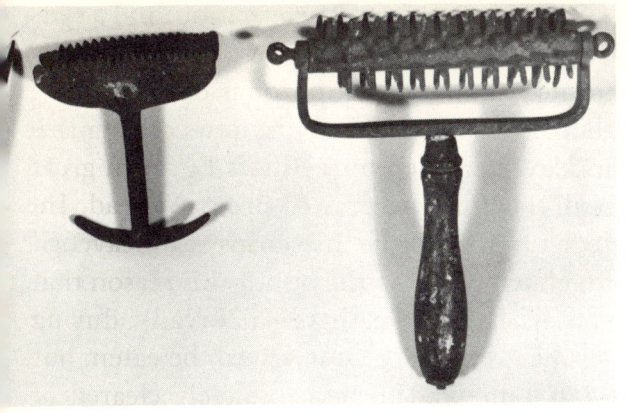

Old European tools for matzah-making. Left: a compass to measure the round matzot. Right and center: wheels to make the tiny perforations in the matzot before baking.

C. Pesach in the East European Shtetl

The destruction of the Second Temple put an end to this form of national celebration. There was no longer a single Temple where all the people could bring their sacrifices. So the people developed a symbolic kind of sacrifice, to remind them of what used to be done in the ancient Temple. An example of this is the placing of the roasted shank bone of a lamb on the seder plate.

The seder itself was developed by the Jewish people during the centuries in which they settled in various countries of the world, after being forced out of their homeland. In those days they felt themselves to be exiles, and the celebration of Pesach gave them hope that they would eventually be redeemed and returned to Jerusalem. The home seder became a home service, in which the theme was that God was a God of freedom and that He would not allow His people to suffer under tyranny forever.

A Jew carrying matzot for delivery in an East European town.

Seder plate, Poland, eighteenth century. Around the rim are engraved the Passover symbols. In the center is a Passover Table with the "Four Sons."

The Passover holiday was one of the chief delights of the Jews of Eastern Europe, for on Pesach they could revive all their historic memories of the past glories of Israel, all their hopes of redemption by a Messiah still to come.

The seder meal, which seems to us now so different from ordinary dinners, actually rep-

77

A Passover plate with the order of the seder around the rim.

resents the way well-to-do people used to eat in ancient times. You may have seen pictures or movies of ancient Babylon, Egypt, Greece or Rome showing important people at their meals; they always reclined on couches and cushions, taking their food from end tables set before them. They began the meal with a drink of wine and some lettuce dipped in a tangy sauce. The seder meal was really the same, except that matzot were eaten instead of bread, and the lettuce or greens were dipped twice instead of once. This type of lavish meal in a relaxed and comfortable atmosphere serves to convey the spirit of freedom and independence associated with the Passover holiday.

A tremendous fuss was made in the Eastern European communities over getting rid of chametz. A single seed of grain found in a pot would make it not *Kosher* for Passover (not "clean" in the religious sense). And if a seed of the harvest from before Pesach blew into a well, that well could not be used during Passover.

The night before Passover, the final cleansing of the home from all chametz was performed. Although the house had already been thoroughly purified, the symbolic ceremony had to be carried out. Bits of bread were actually placed here and there, so that the father, returning from evening prayers, might find them. He would hold a wooden spoon, and with goose-feathers or willow-twigs he would sweep the chametz into the spoon and wrap it up to be burned.

The *charoset* (a dessert-like compound of grated nuts and apples mixed in cinnamon and wine) was usually prepared in large quantity by one well-respected housewife,

Washing Passover dishes in the Mikvah. From a sixteenth century illuminated Haggadah.

Page from an illustrated Haggadah of the fifteenth century showing preparations for Passover.

who then supplied it to the whole community. Each family would donate a few coins for their share, and the money was used for charity. Jews unable to pay for their Passover supplies received everything, including matzot, free of charge.

Passover was a busy and lively time for all; and it was exciting, in addition, for children. The *cheder* (Hebrew school) was only open half-days from the first of Nisan through the fourteenth, and then was closed all eight days of Passover. (Up to about 100 years ago there was no Reform Judaism in Eastern Europe, so everyone observed Pesach for eight days.) The children took part in hunting for chametz, in bringing home the charoset, and running errands. Most of them received new suits or dresses, or at least one or two new things to wear. The youngest in each family had to ask the *arba kushiot* (the four questions) at the seder. One lucky child would find the *afikoman* (a special piece of matzah used for dessert), and would receive a present for returning it. And there was the thrill of waiting to see if Elijah the Prophet would enter and drink his cup of wine!

The four questions were not always as they are now. While the Jews were still in Jerusalem, one question asked was why the sacrificial animal was served on the seder night. But when the Jews were exiled to other lands, there was no sacrificial animal, so this question had to be changed.

The word seder is Hebrew for "order"; it refers to the order in which the Passover ritual is to be conducted. *Haggadah,* the book that contains the Passover home service, is Hebrew for a relating or telling. The Passover Haggadah, first written many hundreds of years ago, tells the story of Israel's deliverance from bondage and explains in detail just how to celebrate the occasion.

Many different Haggadot have been written in the course of time. In each century rabbis

Silver kiddush cup for festivals; London, 1800. Passover Eve scene shows figures standing around table with Paschal Lamb as prescribed in Exodus *12:11.*

79

צְפַרְדֵּעַ דָּם

עָרוֹב כִּנִּים

שְׁחִין דֶּבֶר

אַרְבֶּה בָּרָד

מַכַּת בְּכוֹרוֹת: חֹשֶׁךְ

Illustrations of the ten plagues, from a nineteenth century Polish Haggadah.

and scholars added comments and stories of their own to make the seder more interesting, but each new Haggadah kept the ancient basic ritual.

The seder night came to be a special kind of family night. Jewish families always tried to celebrate the seder together, with young married sons and daughters coming to their parents' homes. Thus, the knowledge that Jews all over the world were sitting together in their family groups at seder made them feel like one big family, the "children of Israel."

D. Pesach in America

The children who attend Jewish schools are aware of the coming of Pesach weeks before. Right after Purim they begin to study the stories connected with the holiday, and also various parts of the Haggadah. They learn the songs of the festival and many Hebrew expressions for use during the celebration, and a few days before Pesach they have a "model" seder in the classroom.

Some temples have a special "model" seder for the parents, to show them how to conduct it at home. Some congregations also have a communal seder for members and their families, in addition to the regular seder that people have in their own homes.

There are many families today that still observe Passover customs brought to this country from Eastern Europe. Reform Jews observe many of these rituals and ceremonies, but they have made some changes in the Haggadah. The following description of a seder in the average American Jewish home today tells us how Reform Jews celebrate Pesach in our time.

The festivities begin with the blessing of holiday candles. The kiddush is said, and the family drinks the first cup of wine. A green vegetable, parsley or lettuce, is then dipped

Silver Passover plate; Austria, 1907. The three compartments are for the three matzot. Decorations: Moses, Aaron, and Miriam and three groups of men, carrying the small dishes for the symbolic foods of the seder.

into salt water and eaten. This is done because the green vegetable signifies the green of springtime, and the salt water the tears shed by the Jews while in bondage. In very ancient times, the well-to-do dipped greens into tasty sauces to start a festive meal. Our people evidently incorporated this custom into the Passover seder, but gave it a new meaning.

The father, or whoever is conducting the

A modern Israeli seder plate.

seder, then breaks the middle one of the three matzot; he manages to hide half of it for the afikoman. This is a word that originally meant dessert; it came to refer to the half of the middle matzah that is hidden. The piece of matzah is hidden for no other reason than to keep the children interested to the end of the seder, when they are all allowed to search for it, and the finder receives whatever reward he asks for, within reason!

The next part of the Haggadah that is read deals with the story of the suffering of our forefathers when they were slaves in Egypt. At one point in the reading some families will open the door to the street, in remembrance of the old-time custom of inviting the poor and hungry to come in and share the seder. Many, of course, do not actually open the door, particularly since so many families live in apartment houses. Instead, people invite guests ahead of time, especially those who

Passover seder in Saigon takes place under combat conditions in Vietnam.

might not have a seder otherwise. In any case the Haggadah passage, inviting the poor to come in, is read.

After this comes the moment for which the youngest child has been eagerly waiting. He (or she) now asks the four questions: "Why is this night different from all other nights?" The child asks why we eat matzot, why we eat

81

This lad is asking the "four questions."

bitter herbs, why we dip one herb in salt water and one in charoset, and why we recline on cushions instead of sitting up.

And the father explains: "We eat matzot because our ancestors, fleeing from Egypt, had no time to bake bread with yeast (or leavening), which causes bread to rise. We eat bitter herbs to remind us of the bitterness of slavery. We dip the parsley in salt water to remind us of the tears our ancestors shed, and in charoset, which has sweetness, to signify the joy of freedom. We lean on cushions because in the past, as slaves, we ate hurriedly, standing or sitting on the ground, but as free people we dine like the free people of old, while reclining on cushions."

He then tells of the four different kinds of sons: the wise one who asks the meaning of the Passover ritual, the rebellious one who asks, "What does it all mean to you," the foolish one who says he can't understand it, the backward one who doesn't understand what is going on but doesn't know how to ask for an explanation. For each one of these, the Haggadah says, the father must give a satisfactory answer, because everyone must come to understand the meaning of Pesach.

What follows in the Haggadah is the story of the freeing of the Jews from Egyptian slavery, after which all the people sing a song of thankfulness, *Dayenu,* meaning "it would have been enough for us."

As the reading of the Haggadah proceeds, the roasted lamb bone is explained as a symbol of the ancient sacrifices, and the matzot as a reminder of our hasty escape from Egyptian slavery. The *maror* (bitter herb), which recalls the bitterness of slavery, is eaten so that every Jew can act as if he himself had tasted what it means to be a slave. He can then all the more feel joy at being free.

After a blessing is recited for Passover, a second cup of wine is drunk. The leader of the seder then distributes pieces of matzah, for which a brachah is said and the matzah is eaten. Now the maror is dipped in the charoset and everybody at the seder says the proper blessing and eats a piece of the bitter herb.

By this time all the symbols of the Pesach have been brought into the seder, and the Passover meal is begun. Some people serve a

A modern matzah-baking machine.

82

A matzah bag contains three compartments for three matzot. The afikoman is taken from the middle matzah. This young man is arranging the matzah bag for the seder.

roasted egg as a start, because they believe the egg is a symbol of life, which fits in with the theme of spring that is connected with Passover. Others say it is because the egg stands for the roasted sacrifice which took place in the Temple in ancient times.

After the meal is eaten, the father tells the children to look for the other half of the broken matzah, the afikoman. The lucky one who finds it is sure of a gift or a special treat, because the piece of matzah he holds is very important. Until the afikoman is distributed and eaten, the meal cannot be considered finished.

After this piece of matzah is broken up and eaten, nothing more is eaten. The people then say the blessings after the festival, and a number of traditional songs are sung, among them the famous *Chad Gadya* (An Only Kid) and "Who Knows One?" Two more cups of wine are drunk and the door is opened for the prophet Elijah to enter. In our tradition it has been the belief that Elijah will be the one who will announce the coming of the Messiah. Of course, he does not come in to drink his cup of wine, but he is understood to be there in spirit.

For hundreds of years every seder all over the world ended with the wish: "Next year in Jerusalem." In most countries, including our own, many Jews still say this at the close of the seder, meaning they hope to hold the next seder in the Holy Land. In Israel, however, Jews do not say this at all, for they are in the Holy Land already.

E. Bringing the Haggadah Up to Date

To anyone, especially a Jew who has been in Israel in springtime, the simple renewing of nature would be something to make a holiday about, even if there were no great historical event to celebrate. The fresh blue of the

The youngest of this family recites the "four questions" at a Passover seder.

Three times a year (Sukkot, Pesach and Shavuot) the Jews of ancient Israel would march on foot to the Holy Temple in Jerusalem. Today in modern Israel, the age-old ceremony is re-enacted. Here modern pilgrims ascend Mt. Zion to the blowing of the shofars.

sky, the blossoming flowers and trees, the air suddenly soft and fragrant, the sparkling sunlight on the blue Mediterranean, on the hurrying River Jordan, or the still waters of lovely Lake Kinneret—how could anyone help but rejoice! But in addition to all this, to have Passover to celebrate in such a time, how truly delightful!

It is not surprising, therefore, that the Israeli towns on this great holiday are filled with jubilation, and the whole country celebrates the festival as one family. Not only do they gave thanks for the freeing of the Jews from ancient bondage, but they are also happy that in Israel their spirit and their minds are liberated, so they can live truly and fully as Jews. The Torah Moses gave the Hebrews is a guide to the good life everywhere, but only in Israel, so far, do the Jews have the opportunity to make it the basis of their legal system.

Many Israelis, especially on the kibbutzim, wrote special Haggadot to express their appreciation of the fact that they had at last come to a land that was free for both the body and mind of the Jews. Of course, Jews are free and equal citizens in other countries, too, especially in America, but only in Israel are the holidays and festivals of our religion part of the *national* life of the country. This is what some Israelis want to tell and sing about on Passover.

It is interesting to note that many American Jews also write new Haggadot, for they, too, have some special things to say about this great holiday. Some wish to point out that Jews should not feel completely safe and happy in their freedom, as if it were assured to them for all time. There is always danger from dictators and their fanatical followers. Others want to remind Jews that everybody must be free before we can enjoy true freedom. If Negroes, Indians or other groups in America are not enjoying true equality, then we must help, they say, to improve their situation. Then we could celebrate Pesach all the

A tiny Oriental Jewess helps prepare for Passover.

more joyously, knowing that there was freedom and equality in *every* home.

Some Haggadot in America include passages to show how the Pesach story influenced the early Americans when we were still part of the British Empire. The Pilgrims and other early immigrants to this country read the Bible regularly. They knew the Pesach story quite well, and when speech-makers wanted to show how evil they thought King George III was, they called him "Pharaoh."

The Passover table.

During the American Revolution some people referred to George Washington as "America's Moses." The symbols of Pesach were even in the minds of Thomas Jefferson, John Adams and Benjamin Franklin, when they were asked to design a seal for the new country of the United States of America. They suggested a picture showing the Hebrews crossing the Sea of Reeds to freedom, with the Egyptians mired in its muddy waters. And they suggested this motto on it: "Rebellion to tyrants is obedience to God." Their idea was not accepted, but the mere fact that it was expressed shows how much the story of Pesach has affected people over the centuries.

A seder in Israel. The girl is spilling drops of wine at the recitation of the "ten plagues."

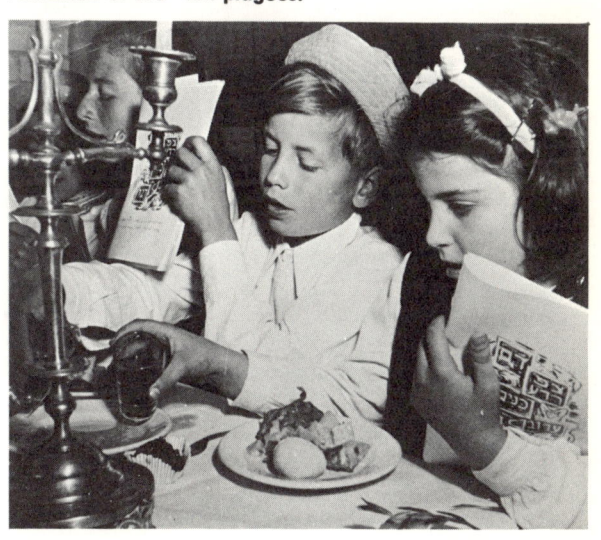

HEBREW HOLIDAY TERMS

PESACH

Pesach	פֶּסַח	Passover
Nissan	נִיסָן	fiirst month
chametz	חָמֵץ	leavened food
matzah	מַצָּה	unleavened bread
maror	מָרוֹר	bitter herbs
charoset	חֲרוֹסֶת	mixture of chopped apples and nuts, wine and cinnamon
afikoman	אֲפִיקוֹמָן	Greek word meaning "dessert"
sayder	סֵדֶר	order (of the festive meal)
kos Eliyahu	כּוֹס אֵלִיָּהוּ	cup of Elijah
mah nishtanah	מַה נִּשְׁתַּנָּה	what is different
dahyaynu	דַּיֵּנוּ	enough for us
arba kushyot	אַרְבַּע קֻשְׁיוֹת	four "questions" (word really means "difficulties") (feer kashes in Yiddish)
Haggadah	הַגָּדָה	the telling (of the Pesach story)
echad mi yoday-ah	אֶחָד מִי יוֹדֵעַ	who knows one (a song)
chad gadyah	חַד גַּדְיָא	an only kid (a song)

YOM HAATZMAUT

A. A Dream Comes True

The people who first came to America left the countries of their birth to build a home in the New World. They brought their languages, which had never before been spoken on America's soil: English, French, Spanish, Dutch, etc. They named places here after places they knew in Europe: New England, New Orleans, New York, New Amsterdam, etc.

It was different when Jews began to return to Palestine to settle, about a hundred years ago. They brought European languages too, but they began to speak again an old language, Hebrew, which had been the national language of Palestine in the days our Hebrew ancestors lived there. And they did not seek to make their new towns and villages like the ones they had left behind in Europe. They wanted most to remake and rebuild Palestine so it could once again become the "land of milk and honey," as it is called in the Bible.

"Return to Palestine" was the dream of the Jews for many centuries. When they said "Next Year in Jerusalem" at the end of the Passover seder, they did not always mean that they felt *they* might settle there some day. To

Proudly the flag of Israel waves on high.

most Jews it was a way of expressing a hope that they would be free at last to live fully as Jews, without being made to suffer for it.

For throughout nearly twenty centuries there were times of great sorrow and persecution for Jews everywhere. Palestine—Jerusalem—Zion! The ancient homeland was a shin-

Members of a Zionist group preparing to go to Palestine. In the center is young David Ben Gurion.

ing star in the distant sky. The vision of the land of Israel as once more the home of the people of Israel helped millions of suffering Jews to hope for the future.

But Europe inflicted on them many *pogroms* (physical attacks), and assigned them only second-class citizenship. Even in America, where the Jews achieved greater freedom and equality than in other parts of the world, even in America there were groups who were hostile toward Jews. It took all their faith in God and Torah, all the hopefulness Jews could muster to keep themselves and Judaism meaningfully alive. Then, as a final blow, came the incredible horror of the Hitler persecutions. It took time but the world was finally shocked into awareness of the helpless situation of the Jews. Through the United Nations the decision was made to return Palestine to the people from whom it had been violently snatched two thousand years before, and thus give Jews, for whom Europe had become a slaughter-house, a chance to build their own state.

Actually Jewish resettlement had begun in Palestine about a hundred years before the vote in the United Nations paved the way for the creation of the State of Israel in 1948. There seemed little hope in the 19th century that Palestine would ever again become a Jewish land; nevertheless, the Russian and East European Jews who went out to Palestine immediately began to rebuild the country as if it were theirs for certain.

During the First World War England agreed, in the Balfour Declaration of November 2, 1917, that Palestine should one day become the national homeland of the Jews. However, the British later decided to hold on to Palestine. The fact that the Arabs claimed Palestine for themselves made it easier for the British to go back on their word. Even when

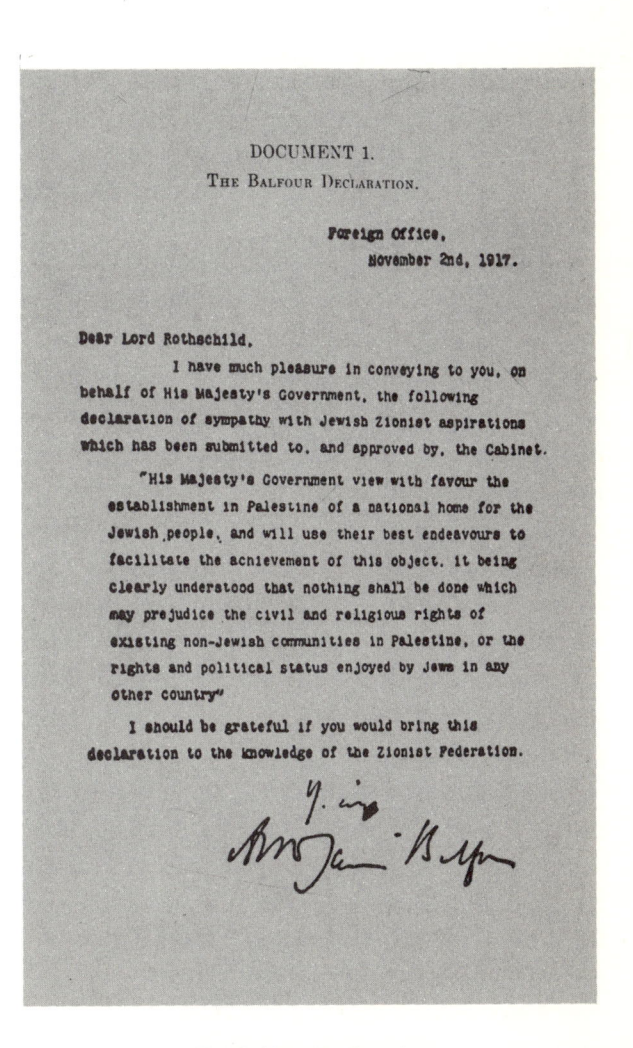

The Balfour Declaration.

An "illegal" ship filled with immigrants seeking to enter Palestine.

the Nazis were rounding up Jews to send to concentration camps and crematoria in Europe, when those who escaped Hitler's dragnet could have found safety if they could get into Palestine, the British refused to permit more than a pitifully small number of Jews to come to Palestine.

After the Hitler wars, many countries realized that it was necessary to do something for the homeless and suffering Jews. The United Nations voted on November 29, 1947 to create a sovereign Jewish state in part of the land of Palestine. England was given six months to prepare the country for the take-over by the Jews of their part, and by the Arabs of theirs.

And so came one of the most glorious days in the long history of the Jews, Iyar the 5th, which in the year 1948 fell on May 14th. This was the day on which the Jews of Israel again became rulers of their own country, after so many centuries of struggle and sorrow.

The gladness was dimmed, however, by the vicious war the Arab leaders immediately started, to drive the Jews out and take away the land that had been voted them. But Israel beat off Arab armies much larger than her own. They fought with their hearts, as did the Maccabees of old, and refused even to think of defeat. And Israel won this war too, bitter and hard though it was.

Their victory was celebrated by the Jewish people the world over, for even though they lived elsewhere they were happy that the wrongs of history were being righted at last. This great joy of Jewish people everywhere is reflected every year in the celebration of the *Yom Haatzmaut* (Independence Day), on the 5th day of the Hebrew month Iyar.

B. A New Holiday to Enjoy

In Israel for three days and nights people stream into the modern city of Jerusalem. The old part of the city with its remnant of the Temple, its ancient streets and arches surviving from Bible times, is now Arab territory and is still closed to Jews. But Israelis and tourists from other lands pour into the newer avenues and the wide streets, whose walls are built with the ancient beautiful "Jerusalem

A torchlight parade on Independence Day.

stone"; they flow into the suburbs and up the hills and on to the plazas of the Hebrew University, the museums, hospitals, synagogues, libraries.

Eating and drinking, singing and dancing in the streets, playing music, parading—everybody celebrates the holiday out in the open. There are concerts, parties and general rejoicing.

On the morning after the great day, there is not a scrap of garbage or litter to be seen in the streets of Jerusalem! It is all cleaned up and cleared away overnight.

Yom Haatzmaut begins in Israel now with a sunset memorial service at the Tomb of Theodor Herzl, the man who, fifty years earlier, started the Jews on the road to making the age-old dream a reality. Twelve huge torches, for the twelve tribes, are lighted, and there is a military salute of one gun for each year of the existence of the State. Strong searchlights form a pyramid of light over Mount Zion, the choir sings, and a great display of fireworks is held.

On the eve of Yom Haatzmaut, a few years ago, a memorable navy pageant was held on

The Declaration of Independence of the State of Israel in Hebrew and in English.

A military parade in Israel on Independence Day.

the sea-front of gaily flag-decked Tel Aviv; it re-enacted the exciting story of the illegal immigration into Palestine, when the British still ruled and kept Jewish immigration down. That same year, two thousand children wearing garlands of flowers marched through the main street of Ramat Gan. In Haifa there was a musical pageant of ancient Israel, with the Haifa City Symphony Orchestra, choir, and soloists. Independence Day greetings were received by the President of Israel from presidents and kings of many nations. A hundred outstanding military men of Israel received the thanks of the State, and four Israel Prizes were awarded for distinguished achievement.

In another year, a parade of military might was held at Tel Aviv, including 300 Israeli Airforce planes, from helicopters and troop transports to supersonic jet fighters. There were tanks, motorized units and armored

Yitzchok Ben Zvi, second President of Israel, visits the tomb of Theodor Herzl at memorial service on Independence Day.

Jew and Arab are learning how to live together in peace and harmony.

units. While the country of Israel does not wish to be considered first and foremost as a military nation, she must give her people the assurance that the government is well prepared to protect the land against possible attack. Israel knows she must show the Arabs that she will maintain and defend her land, her people and her rights.

The excitement of Yom Haatzmaut is not confined to Israel itself. Jews the world over celebrate the great day.

New York especially, with her more than two million Jews, recognizes the day with ceremonies, concerts and meetings. There are special performances and dances in various places. Messages of congratulations are issued by the Mayor of the city and by the Governor of the state.

Jewish children of New York have a wonderful parade and a celebration on the great Mall in Central Park. Special groups dance and sing; there is an exciting program of Israeli music. Thousands of young people, in blue and white, join in a great Israeli dance session on the grass, while a large audience of all ages, waving Israeli and American flags, watch and applaud!

Practically every city that has a fair-sized Jewish population holds some kind of celebration, here in America and in countries all over the world. It is a great day in Jewish history. It is also a great day generally, for the Jews brought with them into the Middle East, where Israel is located, the spirit of democracy and modern, scientific techniques in work and health.

HEBREW HOLIDAY TERMS

YOM HAATZMAUT

Yom Ha-atzma-ut	יוֹם הָעַצְמָאוּת	Independence Day
Hatikvah	הַתִּקְוָה	The Hope (Israel National Anthem)
chalutzim	חֲלוּצִים	pioneers
kibbutz	קִבּוּץ	a farm collective, owned by the people living on it and working it.
Knesset	כְּנֶסֶת	assembly (Israel's Congress)
Iyar	אִיָּר	2nd month of year

LAG BAOMER

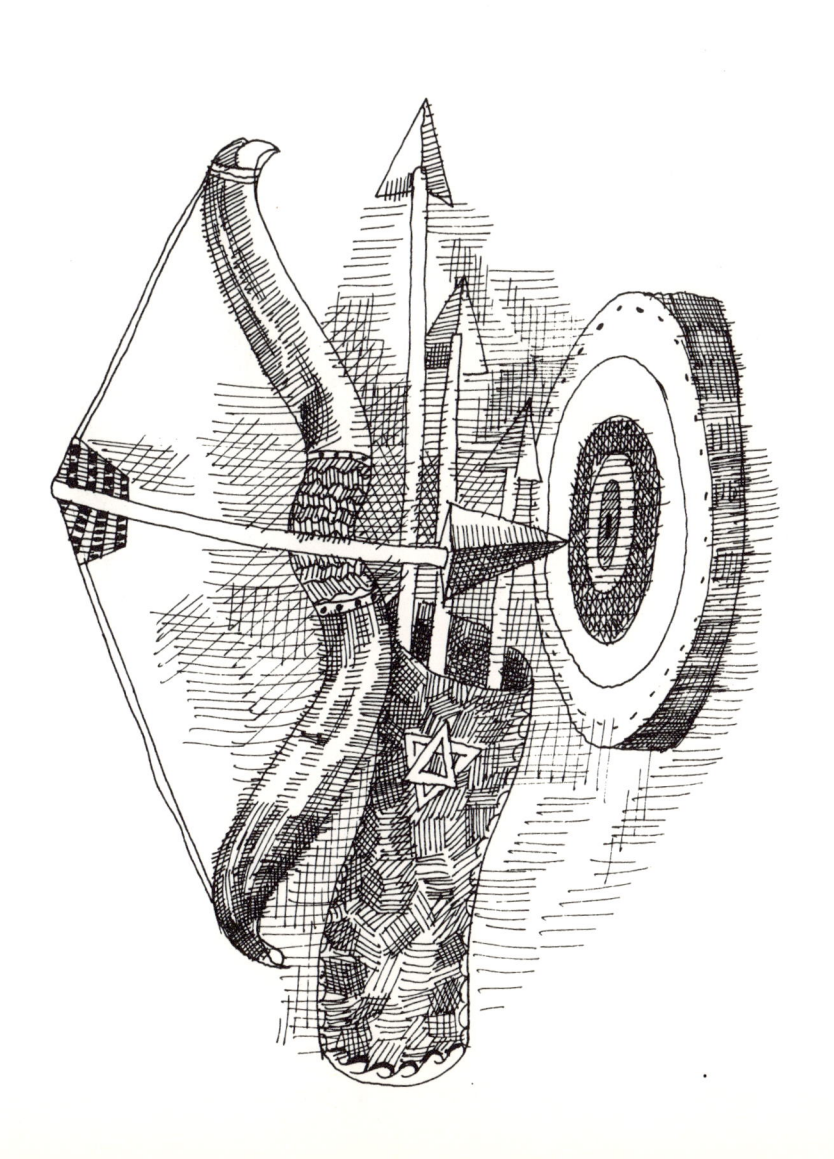

In ancient days when our Hebrew forefathers were farmers in Palestine, they marked the harvest period by bringing a sheaf or measure (an *omer*) of barley to the Temple as a sacrifice. These were solemn and busy days, for the harvest had to be brought in, else the year would be a hard one, with hunger and suffering. And starting from the 2nd day of Passover, when the omer was brought to the Temple, 49 days were counted. After the completion of the 49 days of the omer, adding up to seven weeks, we celebrate the holiday of *Shavuot* (Feast of Weeks.)

So, between the happy days of Passover and the pleasant festival of Shavuot there are seven weeks of serious work and solemn prayers. But it is not one long stretch of seriousness, either. On the thirty-third day of the counting of the omer, the whole mood of the people changes. It is a kind of "relaxation day." Maybe because it can become very tiresome to be without any amusement for so long, the rabbis set this day aside when everybody could be carefree.

This thirty-third day, known better by its Hebrew name *Lag BaOmer* (which means the thirty-third day of the counting of the omer), took on various meanings in the

An ancient stone jug used for storing grain. It can hold an omer.

course of time. It was said to be the anniversary of Simeon bar Yochai's defiance of the Roman Emperor Hadrian's decree forbidding Jews to study the Torah. On this day, too, a plague which had tormented the students of Rabbi Akiba is reported to have stopped suddenly. Lag BaOmer is so much connected with scholars and Torah study, that many call it the Scholar's Holiday, but it also recalls

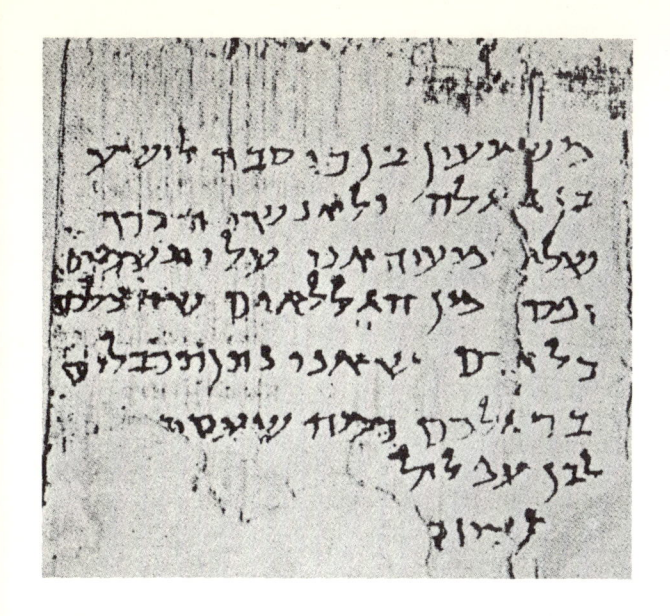

Letter of Simeon Bar Kochba found in Wadi Murubaat in the Desert of Judah (1952).

the days of struggle when the Jews under Bar Kochba revolted against Rome.

These historical ideas became attached to the day as time went by. Customs developed for the observance of Lag BaOmer that had nothing to do with the original reasons for the holiday. Most of the customs applied to Jewish schools, for it gave the children and teachers an opportunity for pleasant outdoor celebration. East European Jewish children used to go out into nearby forests or fields, carrying toy bows and arrows with which they pretended to hunt or fight.

This grew out of the fact that Lag BaOmer

Rabbi Akiba instructing his pupils. From the Sarajevo Haggadah.

was connected in the minds of the Jews with the troubles our people had when Palestine was ruled by Rome. The story says that Jews used to go into the woods, pretending they were going to hunt. Instead they hid Torah scrolls under their cloaks; they sat in circles in some out-of-the-way place, and studied Torah, while one of them acted as look-out to watch for Roman soldiers. But most people who observe Lag BaOmer today don't bother to think very much about the reason why. They simply enjoy it.

In Israel today they make a very gay, exciting holiday of Lag BaOmer. Schools are

Hadrian, Roman emperor (117-138), who suppressed Bar Kochba's revolt against Roman tyranny.

closed, and the children go out on picnics to the woods and hills, usually led by their teachers, where they play games with bows and arrows, sing, dance, have contests and lots of fun.

Older people make pilgrimages to Meron, a village in Galilee, where Rabbi Simeon bar Yochai is buried. On the road one may see

Coin of the Bar Kochba period. The ancient Hebrew reads, "First year of the redemption of Israel" and "Simeon Nasi of Israel."

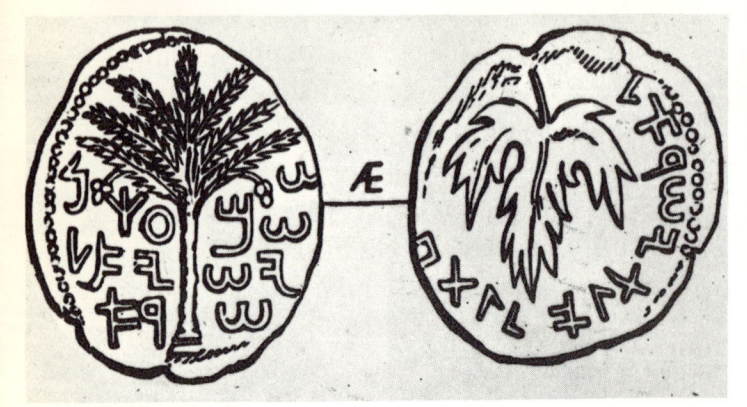

girls and boys and grown-ups as well, going by in laughing groups, trying to hitch a ride up the hill, or bravely hiking the whole way, carrying food, musical instruments and blankets. Most of them will sit around, talking and singing until midnight, after which they will dance around the bonfires as long as they can keep awake. Many songs will be sung about Rabbi Simeon bar Yochai, who is believed to have written the famous book of Jewish mysticism called the *Zohar*. There will also be songs about the courage of Simeon's teacher, Rabbi Akiba, one of the greatest of all the Rabbis.

For the pious and traditional minded Jews there is a great rush to the barber-shops and beauty-parlors on Lag BaOmer, because all the weddings and parties that were delayed by the solemn days of the counting of the omer from Passover on, are celebrated on that one day. Some Jews have made it a custom to

Tiberias, Israel, and the tomb of Rabbi Meir Baal Ha-Nes, member of the Sanhedrin, and pupil of Rabbi Akiba. In the background: the Sea of Galilee.

Hikers to Meron singing and dancing around a bonfire.

give baby boys their very first haircut on Lag BaOmer, so that the child may always remember this holiday.

Among the Jews in the Western countries today, Lag BaOmer is a minor festival, but a merry one. In the all-day Hebrew schools and other tradional schools the children are taken to parks for field days and picnics, and for games and contests. Children in Reform religious schools have fun on that day too, with school parties and assemblies and, weather permitting, outdoor games as well.

Once a year on Lag BaOmer, Safed becomes the scene of fervent religious processions. Here we see a spirited group of Jews making the pilgrimage to the Tomb of Simeon Bar Yohai.

HEBREW HOLIDAY TERMS

LAG BAOMER

Lag BaOmer	לַ"ג בָּעֹמֶר	thirty-third day since the counting of the omer
s'firah	סְפִירָה	counting
omer	עֹמֶר	sheaf, measure
lamed	ל	has value of 30
gimel	ג	has value of 3

SHAVUOT

A. The Changing Nature of Shavuot

Shavuot is the Hebrew word for "weeks" and it comes from a Hebrew root meaning "seven." The idea of "seven" is just right for the holiday of Shavuot, for it is seven weeks of seven days each, from the start of the Palestinian spring harvest season at Pesach time to its end, when the harvest festival of Shavuot was celebrated in ancient times.

In very early times the Jews called this holiday by two names: *Chag Hakatzir* (the Festival of the Grain Harvest), and *Chag Habikkurim* (the Festival of the First Fruits). The "first fruits" in this case referred to the wheat harvest, and for the observance of this festival every farmer would bring a portion of the newly reaped grain to the Temple as an offering. Pilgrims traveled from all over the country to bring these offerings, and to witness the ceremonies of the festival. The Temple service, with much singing of psalms and hymns amid the music of harps and flutes, expressed the thankfulness and joy of the people.

Now you will see just how a holiday changes!

This picture from the world-famous Sarajevo Haggadah shows Moses on Mt. Sinai with the Ten Commandments. Around the foot of the mountain the Israelites await Moses.

For a great many years Shavuot was chiefly a farming festival. Gradually, however, a new meaning began to attach itself to Shavuot,

Mount Sinai, rises majestically above the sands of the desert.

something that the people held to be more important than farming.

For it happened that Moses brought the Hebrews to the foot of Mount Sinai in the month of Sivan, at the very time when the agricultural festival of Shavuot is celebrated! There he gave our forefathers the Torah, the greatest event in our history. As time went on, there were probably many references, during the observance of Chag Habikkurim, to the dramatic story of the giving of the Torah, and the response of the Jews when Moses read them the law. The Jews, our Scriptures tell us, said to Moses, *"Naase v'nishma"* (we will do and obey).

When the Jews, in later centuries, were forced to leave the soil of Palestine, and had to live in towns and cities, the agricultural theme of Shavuot became less important, since few of the people were now engaged in farming. Instead, the giving of the Torah became more important, and it began to displace the idea of the sacrificing of the first fruits. Though the people kept up the connection between farming and Shavuot, they developed a third name for the holiday: *z'man matan toratenu* (the time of the giving of our Law).

This law was the Torah, our great contribution to the world's religious knowledge. Other ancient nations had also developed great ideas in the field of religion, but none of them made as deep an impression upon as many millions of people the world over as the Torah. It appealed to men and women from generation to generation because of its wise laws and helpful teachings as to how people should act toward each other and toward God. And now Shavuot became the holiday for the celebration of the great event, the giving of the Torah to the Children of Israel.

Two Tablets of the Law found in the caves at Bet Shearim, Israel. These carvings date back almost two thousand years.

Ancient jars found in caves at Qumran, containing some of the famous Dead Sea Scrolls.

B. Reform Judaism and Shavuot

Some very old customs became attached to the holiday of Shavuot, and we are not too sure in every case just why. We can understand why people decorate their houses with green leaves and flowers, for it is an agricultural festival and it comes in late spring when the earth is like a garden. But it is not so clear why dairy dishes became the traditional food to be served at Shavuot. Perhaps it's a natural change due to warmer weather. Some rabbis quote a verse from the Bible wherein the Torah is compared to milk and honey, and that may be a reason why we eat these foods on the day the Torah was given.

Certain synagogue customs for Shavuot also developed in olden days. Up to recent times (and in some very traditional communities it is still done), it was the custom on the eve of the festival for older people to go to the

Facsimile of part of a Dead Sea Scroll.

The greatest treasure of the Jewish people, the Torah, crowned in silver and clothed in regal velvet.

house of study (*Bet Hamidrash*) to spend the night reading sections of the Bible, Talmud and other great Jewish works. Next evening, they recited the Psalms of David (it is believed by some that David was born and died on Shavuot). In some synagogues a 24-hour candle was lit on Shavuot, in memory of King David.

A special song, composed almost a thousand years ago, is still sung in some synagogues on Shavuot. It is called *Akdamut Milin* (Before the words), which is a hymn to the glory

A Confirmation ceremony.

of God, to His Torah and to the righteous who study it. The great rabbis will sit on golden thrones, under canopies of light; they will dance and rejoice. For God will grant "abundant peace" to pure and upright men. It is a fitting song for Shavuot because it exults in the blessing that was bestowed upon the Children of Israel when they were selected to receive the Torah.

One of the beautiful Shavuot customs which have come down to us is the reading of the Biblical Book of Ruth in the synagogue. This is done partly because the events of the book occur at the time of the grain harvest in Israel. This book recreates in a delightful way the setting in which the holiday was celebrated in ancient Israel. The Book of Ruth also tells how Ruth the Moabite clung to the Jewish people and the Jewish faith and became the ancestress of the House of David. The story of Ruth thereby symbolizes the spirit of Shavuot, the holiday upon which the Jews accepted the Torah and committed themselves to a life of obedience to God's laws.

As time went on the holiday began to change; some of its customs began to have less and less meaning for modern Jews. Not many were willing to stay home from work in order to attend the synagogue service, and rabbis grew to expect only small congregations at Shavuot prayers.

Then, in about 1810, Reform Rabbis had an idea that was not only inspiring but very practical too. It resulted in bringing large numbers of Jews back into the synagogues for services on Shavuot. They developed a ceremony called Confirmation, and in time it became associated with Shavuot.

Confirmation has a natural relationship with the holiday of the Giving of the Law, for on Shavuot our people confirmed their faith in God and His Torah. After they heard Moses read the law to them, they publicly declared, "All that the Lord has spoken we will do."

A female confirmand.

105

A wood engraving of the Ten Commandments.

The religious movement known as Reform Judaism, which seeks ways of making the Jewish religion meaningful in terms of modern life, wanted a ceremony at which *girls* as well as boys could confirm their faith. For boys, there already existed the *Bar Mitzvah* (Son of the Commandment). But 150 years ago there was nothing in the form of a special ceremony marking a girl's coming of age in the religious sense. So, when Reform worked out the idea of Confirmation for girls as well as boys, and assigned Shavuot as the holiday best suited for this ceremonial, it was hailed with joy, especially by parents of girls. It became more and more popular. Many Conservative congregations also adopted the the custom of Confirmation and they also celebrate it at the Shavuot service. The public Confirmation ceremony for a group of boys and girls takes place usually when the boy or girl is about sixteen, and has completed about three years of additional study and preparation after Bar (or Bat) Mitzvah, during which time their faith has been strengthened by greater knowledge.

Reform religious schools have developed a most interesting pattern or format for this service. There is usually a cantata, often one composed for the occasion, which the Confirmands perform. They also participate in many parts of the service, and may insert special prayers which they have written as part of their preparation for the Confirmation service. The rabbis usually bless each of the Confirmands, who are dressed in ceremonial robes. All the Confirmands make their pledge to "do and obey" the laws of the Torah, just as the Hebrews at the foot of Mount Sinai vowed to Moses about 3,200 year ago. And the Sanctuary is often filled with people at the Shavuot Confirmation Service.

Thus an almost outdated holiday of the past has been developed into a vital new holiday, enriched with present-day thought as well as ancient faith.

A Shavuot pageant in Israel.

A young Israeli farmer bringing in the first fruits.

C. Shavuot in Israel

There is no ceremony of Confirmation as yet in the State of Israel, because there are only a few Reform congregations and these are still very young. Nevertheless, Shavuot is celebrated there with much excitement. Everywhere one sees processions of children and young people, dressed in white and wearing wreaths of flowers! Some carry baskets filled with fruits and vegetables from the farms, while others hold aloft fresh-cut sheaves of barley and wheat. Whatever is grown is displayed with pride at public assemblies and gatherings, and with community dancing and singing.

The holiday is observed with most excitement in the kibbutzim and in the farming areas generally, for there the people feel the special joy of harvesting the crops they themselves planted. They bring in their first fruits, dancing and singing, in gratitude for the marvels of God and nature that supply them with food, and they are proud of their part in making their ancient country fertile again.

Processions in both country and city usually lead to open-air theatres where a pageant is performed, in which old-time ceremonials of Shavuot are combined with customs of modern Israeli life. They show the arrival of pilgrims at the gates of old Jerusalem, where they are met by the elders and the working people, who greet them and lead them to the (imaginary) Temple. The dancers or actors give their baskets of first fruits to the "priests," who place them around the "altar." The songs and music are generally new, composed in the spirit of the new Israel, and the dances have the rhythms and gestures of modern times. Many of the first fruits which they bring are also modern, for Israel now grows many products that were not known to ancient Palestine.

And yet, the new customs that Israelis have brought to Shavuot celebrations have made the holiday more like that of our ancestors, for the Israelis emphasize the agricultural meaning of Shavuot; to them it is a harvest festival once again. Once again it is Chag Hakatzir, that our ancestors of biblical times used to celebrate, even though they did it with different songs and dances.

Influenced by the Israelis, many Jewish communities in other countries have adopted similar celebrations on Shavuot. They also make it a gay, open-air holiday, a happy day in honor of the brave people who have rebuilt Palestine. In cities throughout the United States, Jewish religious schools join to make a *Bikkurim* (first fruits) pageant, reminding us that our ancestors were once farmers, and that Jews in Israel are again making fertile the soil where our people and religion grew and developed.

HEBREW HOLIDAY TERMS

FOR SHAVUOT

Shavuot	שָׁבוּעוֹת	weeks
z'man matan toratenu	זְמַן מַתַּן תּוֹרָתֵנוּ	time of the giving of our Torah
Chag Habikurim	חַג הַבִּכּוּרִים	the Festival of First Fruits
s'firah	סְפִירָה	counting (of the omer)
Chag Hakatzir	חַג הַקָּצִיר	the Harvest Festival

SHABBAT

A. Shabbat and Democracy

Would you agree that one of the greatest contributions to democracy is contained in the Fourth Commandment?

"Remember the Sabbath day, to keep it holy." Why is this "democracy"?

What, after all, has the Sabbath to do with democracy?

But if we keep in mind that democracy has to do with, among other things, the equal treatment of all people, and the greatest good to the greatest number, then the connection begins to be clear!

The Fourth Commandment establishes the Sabbath as a day of rest.

It is hard to imagine this, but once upon a time *every* day was a working day. This Commandment was the first law that forbade all work on every seventh day. So this law was for the benefit of those who did the hard work of the world.

Before the time of the Exodus from Egypt and the giving of the Torah, there was no regular rest day for servants, slaves, hired workers, or animals. Every hired hand or self-employed person was expected to work every day, and for long hours.

Blessings for candle-lighting for Sabbath and holidays, from an 18th-century Italian prayer book. Note the interesting Sabbath lamp and the Italian translation.

In the whole world outside the Jewish faith, work without rest was the general condition of man and beast. When Jews adopted the Sabbath, as the Torah commanded them to, non-Jews considered them lazy! Some famous people in ancient Greece and Rome made unfriendly remarks about the Jewish custom of working only six days. But as time went on, the rest of the world began to realize that a day of rest improved the health and refreshed the working strength of all. So other peoples set aside a day of rest each week. The Christians, for instance, made Sunday a holy day and the Mohammedans picked Friday.

The beauty of the Hebrew Sabbath was not only that it compelled masters and employers to give their workers a day of rest, but that the law applied to the home as well. Housewives, whose work in primitive times was indeed hard and endless, were also freed by the Sabbath from their heavy tasks. No cooking was done on the Sabbath. The meals for that day were prepared on Friday. Nor did the mercy of the Sabbath end there. Animals which had become the servants of mankind were also granted this day for rest and peace. Neither the donkey nor the ox nor any other beast was to be made to work on *Shabbat*. If they could have understood this, imagine how grateful they would have felt!

The Sabbath law holds benefits for the wealthy also, if they follow the rules for the day, for it bids them rest from their concentration on business. It invites them to realize and enjoy the spiritual side of life.

For all people the Sabbath is a blessing. It leaves the mind free to think, and the heart free to feel and to express itself. The Sabbath law from the very beginning brought a sense of blessedness, of freedom and exultation.

It is for these reasons that the Sabbath commandment is regarded as democratic; it was given for *all* people to enjoy. Our ancestors, by adopting this day, made the first

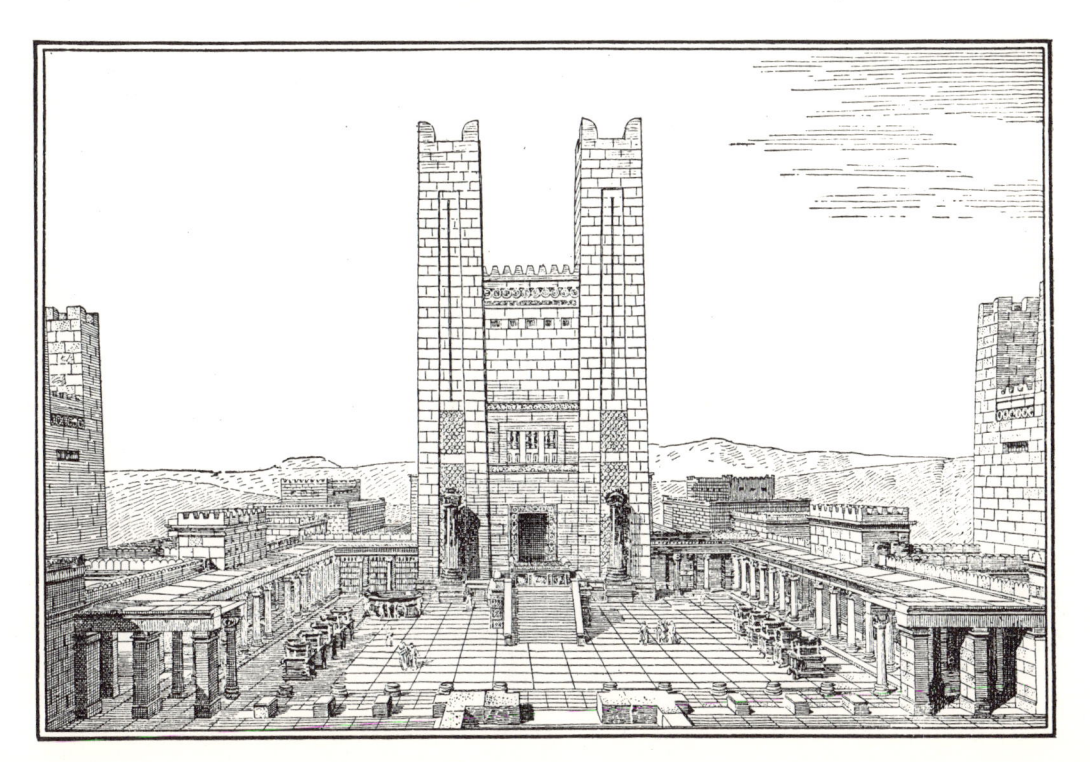

A reconstruction of the Court of Priests in the ancient temple.

A ninth century Persian Sabbath lamp.

move to cut the work week for all workers, men and women.

B. Shabbat in Ancient Times

In ancient Jerusalem, when the city was comparatively small, many Jews went to the Temple of Solomon every Sabbath. The people set aside work and business from sunset on the sixth day until sunset on the seventh day.

Jews living outside of Jerusalem, too far off to walk to the Temple, kept Sabbath on their own. We have no record of the exact ways in which they did this, but we do know that when the Temple was destroyed in 586 B.C.E. and the Jews were brought to Babylon as captives, the Sabbath became almost immediately the most important holiday of the year. Every week the Jews met to give praise to the Lord and to study His Torah. When Ezra, the Scribe, left Babylon and came to Jerusalem, one of the things that disturbed him most was finding the Jews of Palestine so ignorant of Torah and so neglectful of the Sabbath. He and Nehemiah had a difficult job teaching them how to observe the Sabbath.

More and more, the Sabbath day became the day of God, a Holy Day, as well as a day of complete rest. But Jews sometimes disagreed as to the best way to honor the Sabbath. A group of Jews later known as Karaites, said that people should keep very strictly to the Sabbath laws. They thought people should stay close to home on that day and that it was wrong to make a fire or any light during Shabbat. Their very strict views were not acceptable, however, to most Jews. Most of our people felt it was a day for spiritual happiness. How could the day have its true purpose of rejoicing in God, they asked, if people made themselves miserable to observe it? The vast majority of the Jews accepted the view of the more liberal teachers of Judaism. The Sabbath was for life, and for the glory of God; therefore it was a day for spiritual enjoyment. And, if a person's life or health was endangered, it was fully permitted to break the laws of the Sabbath.

C. Shabbat is Gladness

The gladness with which the Sabbath was

A nineteenth century German embroidered cloth Challah cover.

These 18th-century candlesticks, made in Germany, have scenes from the Bible on their bases.

greeted is described in songs and poems. It is compared to the joy of a bridegroom greeting his bride. The Sabbath day is often referred to as *Shabbat Hamalkah* (the Princess Sabbath).

In the days when a large number of Jews lived in Europe, our people prepared all their food for Sabbath on Friday or even earlier. On Friday evening, at nightfall, the mother lit and blessed the Sabbath candles, and the father and sons went to synagogue. There, during the Sabbath services, an old song was sung: "Come, my friend, to meet the bride; let us welcome the Sabbath." The Kiddush was chanted over a goblet of wine and the evening prayers were recited.

At home, when they returned, they found a clean white cloth covering the table; this was not removed after the meal but remained on the table until the end of the Sabbath next evening. The father then blessed the children, and praised his wife by reciting some verses of the Book of Proverbs which give honor to the "woman of valor" who keeps house, brings up the children, and holds the family together. The lighted candles shone while the father said Kiddush over the wine, and lit up the scene as he distributed pieces of challah to the family. The blessing for bread was said, and the challah was eaten.

At the synagogue the following morning the service included the reading of the weekly portion of the Torah, and the *Haftarah*, a selection from the books of the Prophets connected with that week's portion of the Torah.

When the first three stars appeared at night, came the formal ending of the Sabbath. The ceremony of *Havdalah* (separation) was recited over wine, and a special twisted candle was lighted. The father recited blessings on the Lord Who brought the holy day into our

Torah Scroll, Germany, 1700.

Spicebox, braided candle, and wine cup used at the Havdalah ceremony.

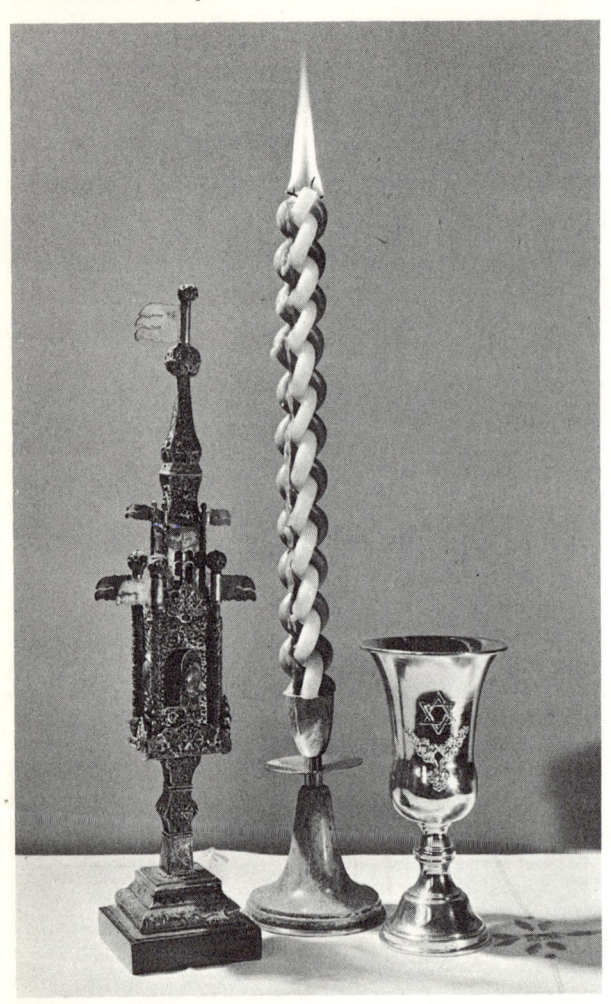

31:17, "It is a sign between Me and the children of Israel forever."

Because they had this feeling that Shabbat was more than a rest day, that it was a day "hallowed unto the Lord," the Jews of old sought to make it as different and as pleasant as possible. They set aside certain foods for the day, such as challah, wine, *gefilte* (stuffed) fish. They lit Sabbath candles to usher the day in and the Havdalah candle to see the Sabbath depart. They saved the best, white tablecloth for serving the Sabbath meal.

Everything connected with the Sabbath was done as artistically as possible. The candlesticks were as fine as the family could afford. The spice-box used in the Havdalah ceremony was often a work of art, and the cover for the challah loaves was usually sewn and embroidered with all the reverence and artistry of the housewife.

When the Jews lived in Europe, especially in the time of the ghetto, Shabbat morning was for worship at the neighborhood synagogue. This was true also of the early Jewish communities in the United States, in the times of our grandparents and great-grandparents. The family went to synagogue, returned for the Sabbath meal, and then rested. Later, everybody went walking if the day was pleasant. Jews would gather with the

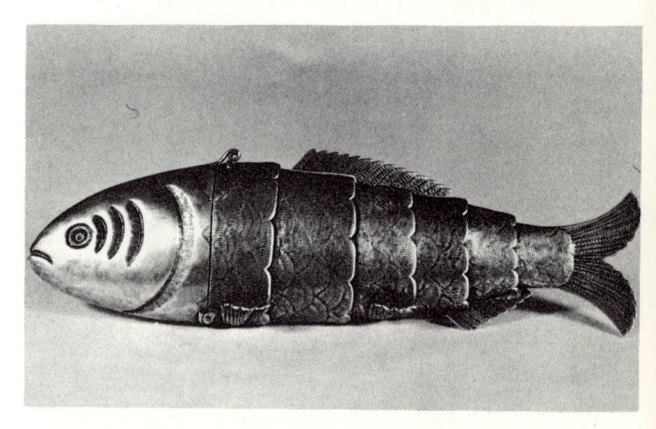

lives and Who separated the Sabbath from the ordinary weekdays. The wine was made to spill over, and the Havdalah candle was put out by dipping it in the overflow.

In Eastern Europe, the traditional Sabbath was kept with great attention to the details of the laws of the Talmud. Many beautiful tales are told of sacrifices made by poor families in order to keep the Sabbath holy, since it was the only holiday for which each Jew was personally responsible, and which he could keep by himself for the glory of God. He felt the Sabbath to be a special covenant between himself and the God of Israel, for it says in Exodus

A silver spicebox in the form of a fish—symbol of fertility and abundance—made in the 18th century.

A porcelain plate used for the Havdalah ceremony, made in 19th-century Germany.

rabbi, or some other learned person, to spend an hour or so reading and discussing one of the important Hebrew books of our religion.

For many Jews, rich or poor, Sabbath was a time for spiritual interests. Thoughts of business or work were put aside. The work-a-day weekdays were the time for fuss and bother. The Sabbath was the time to remember that man was created "little lower than the angels."

D. Shabbat Observance in Our Time

Keeping the Sabbath in the manner we have just described was not very difficult when Jews lived in wholly Jewish communities. It was part of the pattern of living. *All* stores, *all* shops were closed on the Sabbath, for in the ghetto all businesses were Jewish owned. A person who did *not* do what all Jews were doing stood out like a sore thumb. Sabbath, therefore, became part of the very idea of being Jewish. It was so much a part of Jewishness that a great Jewish thinker, Achad Ha-am, was able to say, about seventy-five years ago, "More than Israel has kept the Sabbath, the Sabbath has kept Israel."

But it became increasingly difficult to keep the Sabbath when the Jews were freed from the ghettos and came to live in mixed communities. In the non-Jewish world the day of Shabbat was simply Saturday, just another working day. (This was before the five-day week.) Many of the stores in the neighborhoods the Jews lived in were owned by non-Jews who kept their stores open; and if a store was owned by a Jew, the majority of the customers were non-Jews who usually did most of the family shopping and marketing on Saturday. Many Jewish store-owners therefore began to stay open on Saturday. In general, most of the shops and factories of those days, when Jews began to move into non-Jewish areas, were owned by non-Jews, so most businesses were open on Saturday.

Jewish children attended the public schools,

Blessed art Thou, O Lord our God, King of the universe, who hast sanctified us by Thy laws and commanded us to kindle the Sabbath light.

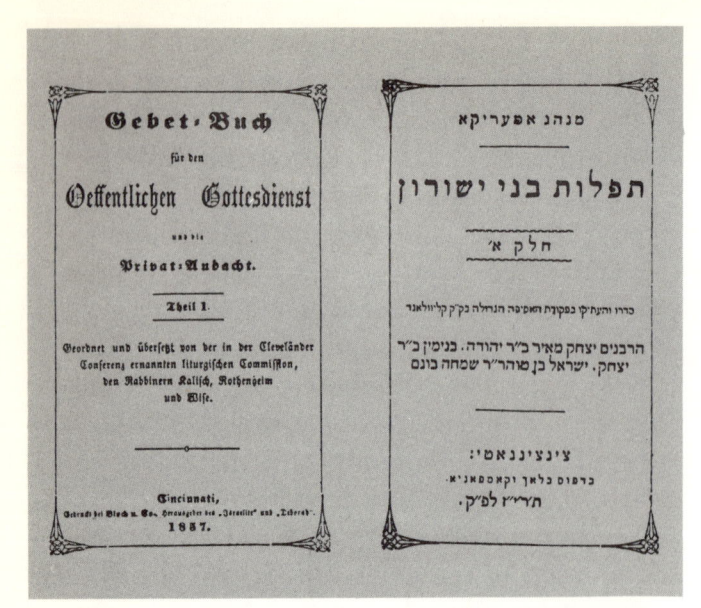

Title page of the first Reform prayer book to appear in America. It was prepared by a commission consisting of Rabbis Kalish, Wise and Rothenheim, and was issued in English, German and Hebrew.

when ghetto restrictions were lifted, and in many European countries the schools were open six days a week, including Saturdays. (In Israel today, schools are open six days a week, including Sunday. There, Shabbat is the day off.)

Families often lived quite a distance from the nearest synagogue. In many cases, it was much too far to walk. The rules for Sabbath, which the rabbis had set a long time before, forbade riding on the Sabbath. Jews who wanted to attend services on Friday evening or Saturday morning, therefore, were unable to do so, unless they were able to walk a great distance and could start the trek early enough. And the majority of Jewish men were obliged to work for their living on the Sabbath, or else be without jobs.

These are just a few of the problems that arose when the Jews were emancipated (freed from the oppressive government laws).

Some very traditional rabbis, who are referred to as Orthodox, insisted that there was but one way to be a Jew: you had to follow *every* ruling that had been made in the past, especially those which Jews had been observing in the ghettos.

But there were many other rabbis who came to believe that it was time to make some new rulings for the Sabbath, as well as for other holidays and Jewish observances. Jewish religious laws should be changed, re-formed, to *help* people to be Jewish, they said, not make it more difficult. These rabbis were called Reform rabbis. Let people ride to the synagogue, they said; at least then they would be *in* the synagogue!

If it was very difficult to attend services on Saturday morning, then it was necessary to select a time when families *could* come. The time that Reform rabbis favored was Friday night, after supper. The *Erev Shabbat* service in the ghettos used to be held early Friday night, it was for men mostly. The late Friday night services that Reform rabbis introduced made it possible for families to attend together.

Changes in Sabbath customs and ceremonies were also made by some traditional groups, after the Reform Movement had paved the way. Conservative and other liberal groups, which came into being after the Reform Movement, also adopted new ways in which to express their Judaism.

Reading the Torah on the Sabbath.

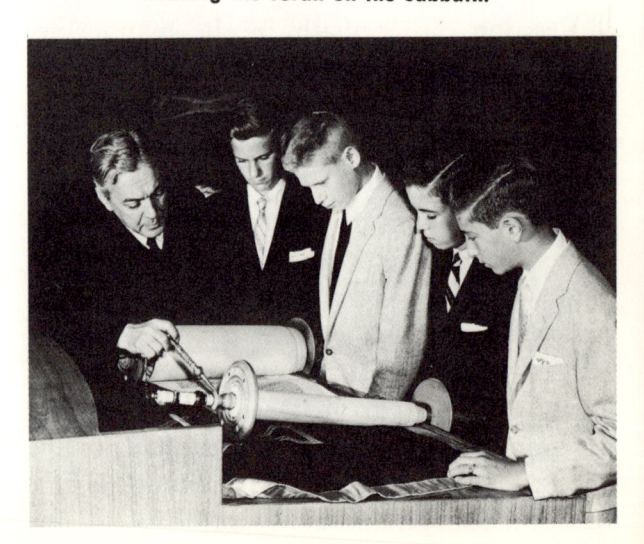

It should be noted, however, that all Jewish groups tried to retain as much of the essence of the Sabbath as they could. As far as Reform Judaism is concerned, the idea has been to devote as much of the day as possible to spiritual pursuits. This can take the form of a service at the synagogue; an *Oneg Shabbat* (an informal gathering after a service that helps give one the *joy of the Sabbath*); occasional Saturday afternoon discussion groups; a home service before the Friday night meal, which includes the lighting of candles and the saying (or chanting) of the kiddush; the reading of the Bible or other important Jewish books.

Reform does not say that one *must* do all of these things; Reform Rabbis and educators suggest that a modern Jew can make the Sabbath meaningful in these Jewish ways, and should certainly seek to make it different from the work-a-day week.

E. Shabbat in Israel

Nowadays it is perhaps only in the State of Israel that the Sabbath can be entirely observed, for there the vast majority of the people of the country are Jewish. The Sabbath can therefore be a country-wide holiday. In Israel, all business stops on the Sabbath. Buses and trains go off duty; offices, stores, factories, schools, theatres are closed and empty. If you plan to go anywhere over the Sabbath, and do not start before two o'clock on Friday, you are in trouble, unless you drive your own car! Even this is disapproved by many people, and in some extremely religious communities cars are not allowed to pass through, once the Sabbath has begun.

This matter of not riding on the Sabbath, and having all business closed down, has created problems in Israel. Some Israelis also think the old ghetto laws for the Sabbath need to be changed. They think modern life requires a time for recreation and the renewal of one's energies, and since there is only one free day, they want to be able "to go places and do things." But the strict religionists are opposed; they fear that Sabbath will become merely a day of recreation, without any spiritual meaning at all.

Sometimes there are demonstrations or clashes because of the opposing ideas. But in time the Israelis will work out a solution to this problem, as they have to so many others.

On Friday, all the flowers at the florists are likely to be bought up, for it has become the

A Sabbath scene on a religious kibbutz in Israel. The Sabbath is a time for study and rest.

Official car announcing the Sabbath. Tel Aviv, Israel.

An Oneg Shabbat walk in Israel.

custom to bring flowers home in honor of Sabbath. Many Israelis have made the Oneg Shabbat part of their life. The Oneg was in fact begun in Palestine, before the State was founded, at the inspiration of the great Hebrew poet of our time, Chaim Nachman Bialik. These Israelis now set aside part of Sabbath afternoon for peaceful and pleasant discussion, or even for more serious talk, and for singing and refreshments.

In Israel one can feel Sabbath in the air. It is the time for a festive meal at home with friends. It is a time to visit, to walk and talk, and to enjoy the goodness of God's world.

F. Shabbat in the Synagogue

For a long time the high point in the observance of the Sabbath has been the worship service at the synagogue. And one of the most important parts of the Sabbath service is the Torah-reading. For each week there is a special *Sidrah* (portion) to be read. The very first portion, the beginning of the Book of Genesis, is always read on the first Sabbath after Simchat Torah. This portion starts with the word *B'reshit* (In the beginning). This Sabbath is referred to, therefore, as *Shabbat B'reshit*.

Some Sabbaths have special names. For instance, there is *Shabbat Shirah* (the Sabbath of Song). This is the Sabbath when the Torah portion *B'shalach* is read, for it contains a poem, "The Song of Moses," which tells how Moses led the Jews out of Egypt.

Shabbat Shekalim (the Sabbath of Shekels) is a reminder of the half shekel tax that Jews in Temple times had to pay. The call for the payment of this tax was made on the first day of the Hebrew month Adar. On the Sabbath before this date, a special reading of Exodus 30:11-16 is held, in which Moses calls on the Hebrews to make this offering to the Lord.

There are other Sabbaths that have special names because they are connected with holidays. The Sabbath that falls within the festi-

Moroccan Jews in the courtyard of their synagogue during Sabbath morning services.

val of Chanukah is called *Shabbat Chanukah*, and the Sabbath before Passover is known as *Shabbat Hagadol* (the Great Sabbath), while the Sabbath before Purim is *Shabbat Zachor* (the Sabbath of Remembrance). The *Maftir* reading for Shabbat Zachor tells of Israel's war against Amalek after the Exodus from Egypt and begins with the word *Zachor* (Remember.)

Another special Sabbath is the solemn and serious one that we call *Shabbat Shuvah* (the Sabbath of Return). This is reserved for the Sabbath that falls between Rosh Hashanah and Yom Kippur. The word *Shuvah* means return in the religious sense of giving up one's evil or mean ways and returning to the ways of God. Shuvah is the first word of the Haftarah reading on that Sabbath, from the Prophet Hosea, chapter 14, verses 2-10.

If the Sabbath fell on the night of a new moon, the old-time Jews called it *Shabbat Rosh Chodesh* (the Sabbath of the beginning of the month). Special prayers are still said in honor of this occasion by those Jews who follow the ancient traditions closely. The custom arose in ancient Hebrew times when the people praised the Lord for the order and regularity of His universe. The ceremony of blessing the

An eighteenth century European engraving showing the Blessing of the New Moon.

new moon was important to the ancient Jews for still another reason; they had no other calendar, and kept track of the seasons by counting the 29½ days after each new moon as one month. The Rosh Chodesh blessing announced the start of a new moon and the people could begin their count at the right time.

HEBREW HOLIDAY TERMS

SHABBAT

erev Shabbat	עֶרֶב שַׁבָּת	on the eve of the Sabbath
birkat hanerot	בִּרְכַּת הַנֵּרוֹת	blessing of the candles
Kiddush	קִדּוּשׁ	consecrating, or making holy
b'rachah	בְּרָכָה	a blessing
shacharit	שַׁחֲרִית	morning prayer service
t'filah	תְּפִלָּה	prayer
aliyah	עֲלִיָּה	going up (to the Torah)
siddur	סִדּוּר	prayerbook
Shabbat shalom	שַׁבָּת שָׁלוֹם	a peaceful Sabbath! (greeting on Sabbath)
oneg Shabbat	עֹנֶג שַׁבָּת	joy in the Sabbath
sidrah	סִדְרָה	Torah portion of the week
kaddish	קַדִּישׁ	prayer for the dead
m'nuchah	מְנוּחָה	rest
havdalah	הַבְדָּלָה	separation (prayer at end of Sabbath)
birkat hamazon	בִּרְכַּת הַמָּזוֹן	blessing of the food (after Sabbath meal)

TISHAH B'AV

A. Tishah B'av

Every nation in human history has had tragic days on which calamities befell them. Wars were lost; great floods, or great fires, or terrible plagues took place.

Most peoples, including the Jews, prefer to commemorate happy events. But the Jews observe sad occasions as well. One such holiday is many hundreds of years old. It is called *Tishah B'Av* (the 9th day of the Hebrew month of Av), and recalls the tragic happenings that took place on that day. First, the Babylonians, and then, 650 years later, the Romans, each time on the 9th day of Av, defeated the Jews and destroyed the Temple in Jerusalem.

It was a painful memory, and life would have been more pleasant if the Jews could have forgotten it. But they wanted to remember. Not because they liked to think of sad events, but because the Temple had meant so much to them in the past. It had become a symbol of our religion; it was regarded as the "House of God." When the Babylonians destroyed the first Temple, the Jews built a second one. But after the Romans destroyed that one, the Jews could not rebuild it because the conquerors exiled them from Jerusalem and turned the city into a pagan Roman town.

The Jews afterwards worshipped God in their synagogues, but wherever they lived and no matter how contented they felt otherwise, on Tishah B'Av they fasted. People who had never seen Jerusalem or the Temple wept

Ruins of an ancient synagogue at Kfar Nahum date back to the second and third century C.E.

A copy of the carving on the Arch of Titus, showing the menorah and other furniture of the Temple being carried in triumph through the streets of Rome.

with grief over the loss, because every Jew who took his Judaism seriously, in days gone by, felt that Zion was part of his soul. Without it, he felt something missing in his life.

After the first destruction, when the Jews of the Kingdom of Judah were taken captive and exiled to Babylonia, they gathered "by the waters of Babylon" and wept over the loss of the Temple. In their mind's eye they saw again the sorrowful scene of King Nebuchadnezzar's Babylonians burning down the Temple of Solomon. When the Temple was rebuilt, there was for a time no need for sorrow. But after the Roman destruction the sad memory was revived. Those who saw it could never forget the streets being torn up

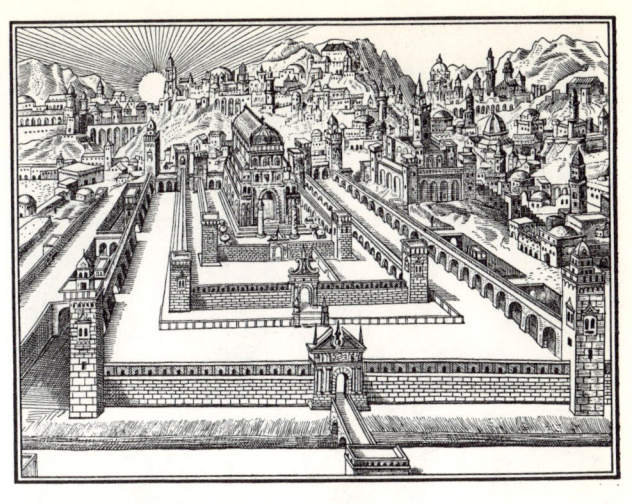

An artist's idea of the Bet Hamikdash, the Temple in Jerusalem. The large area, the Temple Mount, was surrounded by a wall.

by the Romans, while Jews by the thousand were transported as slaves to Rome and other parts of the Roman Empire.

For hundreds of years Jews fasted on the ninth day of Av, and came together in their synagogues to mourn for the Temple of old. They took off their shoes and sat down on the floor, bowing their heads low. At first, to show their intense grief, they did not wear their customary *tallit* (prayer-shawl) or *t'fillin* (special little boxes worn on the arm and forehead for purposes of prayer). They sang mournful prayers and psalms all day, under dim lights. Later, for the afternoon prayers, they put on the tallit and t'fillin to show their faith in God's promise to Abraham that some day his descendants would dwell in multitudes in Palestine.

The Sabbath before Tishah B'Av is called *Shabbat Chazon* (the Sabbath of Vision). The name comes from the first word of the Haftarah reading for that Sabbath, Chazon, meaning vision. It deals with the vision of destruction that the prophet Isaiah foresaw for Jerusalem.

At the Tishah B'Av service itself, the Biblical selection is the Book of Lamentations. This was believed to have been written by the

Wearing t'fillin at morning prayer. The box on the forehead, fulfilling the commandment "And they shall be for frontlets between thine eyes," contains passages from the Torah.

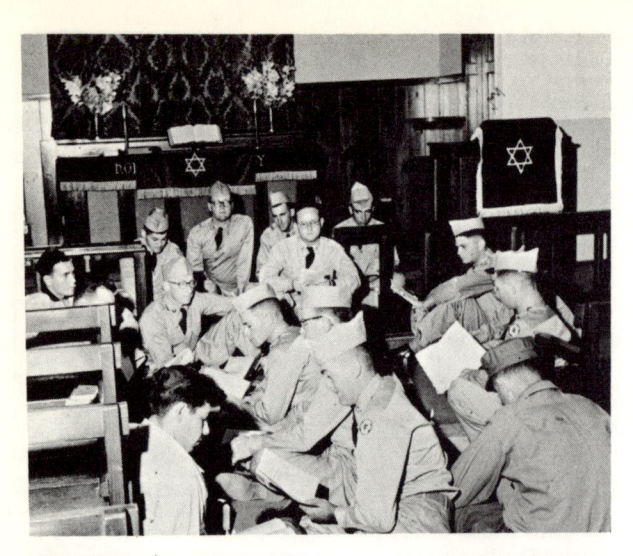

Tishah B'Av service at an army camp in the United States.

great prophet Jeremiah, but scholars now say it was composed by others. But the authorship is not important; Lamentations is read because it deals mostly with the destruction of Jerusalem and the Temple.

The mood of the day was always a sad one, but it was not one of complete despair. The people still could look to the future. There was always the hope that, with the help of God, the Jews would one day return and again make Jerusalem their city, and Mount Zion a holy place. They never really gave up hope.

But the holiday of Tishah B'Av has become a problem for many modern Jews. They are sad about the destruction of the Temple, but they know quite well that even though Jews could build a new Temple in Jerusalem now there is no real need for it. We worship in local synagogues; we do not need a central Temple, nor could we possibly return to the ancient system of sacrifices that were offered there. After all, they point out, there are over two million Jews in Israel today, and the capital of the country is once again Jerusalem. So they do not think it necessary to fast or to set the ninth of Av aside as a day of mourning. Instead, some feel that this holiday should express our gratitude and joy that there is a Jewish land once more.

But there are Jews who cannot forget the sorrows of our past. And so, as Jews have done for hundreds of years, they go to their synagogues, to fast and to bewail the burning of the First and Second Temples, and the scattering of our people in exile all over the world. Even in the modern State of Israel, this tragic day in our people's history is commemorated. At sundown, on the evening before, cinemas and theatres are closed; there is complete stillness in many parts of the land, as people go to the synagogue and begin the long, sad chanting of the Book of Lamentations. Many keep strict fast, though it is not compulsory.

It is true, however, that a considerable part of the population does not fast or pray on this day. Only the most pious and tradition-

The Western Wall in the Old City of Jerusalem is all that remains of the Second Temple.

An aerial view of the Tomb of King David on Mount Zion.

minded continue this observance.

Formerly, pious Jews would go to the Wailing Wall, the last remaining piece of the wall of the ancient Temple, to pray all day. But since this is now in the territory of the State of Jordan, which does not permit Jews to enter the country from Israel, these people come together instead at the tomb of King David on Mount Zion.

HEBREW HOLIDAY TERMS

TISHAH B'AV

Tishah B'Av	תִּשְׁעָה בְּאָב	ninth day of the month of Av
tallit	טַלִּית	prayer shawl

YOM HAZICARON

It is too early to tell yet whether *Yom Hazicaron* (the Day of Remembrance) will become a great day of observance like the other festivals we celebrate, for it is a newly developed holiday. It grew up in recent years in order to remember and honor the six million Jews who were killed during the *Shoah* (the holocaust or Hitler terror) of 1933-45.

Of all the attacks upon Jews that took place in history, this was by far the worst. Simply because they were Jews—and it did not matter whether they were tradition-minded or liberal or Reform in their practice of Judaism or good or bad as people—the Nazis sought to do away with all of them. Rich or poor, brilliant or dull, talented or ordinary, righteous or sinner, so long as they were Jews, the followers of Hitler hunted them down throughout Europe.

Since most of the countries of Europe had fallen to Nazi Germany, there were few places the Jews could escape to. Some Jews succeeded, but most were hopelessly trapped. Some who died had had no idea what their fate was to be, else they would have attempted to flee to life and freedom in time. But they remained in Europe. They could not imagine that any human beings in the 20th century

The Warsaw monument in memory of Six Million martyred Jews.

A close-up view of the Warsaw Monument.

could be so evil, so lacking in any moral feelings as to wish to destroy a whole people simply for being Jews. But it happened; it was all too real.

Jewish leaders felt that these martyrs could not be left unsung, unremembered. Therefore, some years ago, Jews began to include a special prayer in the Haggadah that is read on Pesach, in memory of the Six Million. In many homes during the seder, usually at the time the door is opened for *Eliyahu Hanavi*, the people sing *Ani Ma-amin* (I Believe). This is a song based on the creed of the great philosopher Maimonides, expressing his faith that the Messiah will yet come. It is sung because a great many of the Six Million went to their death singing this very song. It was their way of showing the Nazis and the world that they had faith in God, faith that there would be a Day of Judgment for the murderers, and a time of justice and peace for the righteous.

Jews also hold memorial meetings on the twenty-seventh of Nisan in honor of the Warsaw Ghetto fighters, who in 1943 raised the banner of revolt against the Nazis. Many large gatherings are held all over the world to commemorate this event.

In Israel the government established a memorial museum for the Six Million, called the *Yad Vashem,* which collects all documents and information having to do with the Shoah. Millions of visitors from all over the world have come there to pay their respects to those of our people who fell victim to the Nazis. The museum also collects information about *non-Jews* who helped to save Jews out of the hands of the German monsters. These names

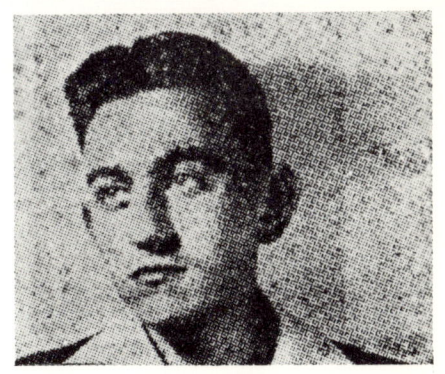

Michal Kelpfisz, a hero who was killed in the heroic defense of the Warsaw Ghetto.

are publicized so that our people and all the world will know that there were brave and decent non-Jews who, at the risk of their own lives, stood up for humanity and civilization.

The people of Israel have been working to consecrate the 4th day of Iyar, the day before Yom Haatzmaut, as a specific day of memorial to the Shoah martyrs. Called Yom Hazicaron, it is a day to be observed with special meetings and ceremonies to keep alive the memory of those who died, and to pledge to continue the faith and culture which was the mark and honor of the people whom Hitler tried to destroy.

The Yad Vashem Memorial Museum in Israel.

HEBREW HOLIDAY TERMS

YOM HAZICARON

Yom Hazicaron	יוֹם הַזִכָּרוֹן	the Day of Remembrance
Shoah	שׁוֹאָה	The Holocaust

LOOKING BACK OVER THE HOLIDAY YEAR

And so, together, we have watched a whole year of Jewish holidays go by. Actually, that's not quite the right way to put it—we didn't just sit back and watch as we read this book. We danced, we sang, we celebrated the festivals in all kinds of ways, with games and talk and plays, with food and parties and all sorts of fun.

They're lively occasions, the Jewish holidays, and they were made for enjoyment. Maybe not the wild, horn-tootin' kind of revelry that is sometimes shown in the movies and on television, but they certainly give us a chance to get together as Jews and frolic a little, or at least to do something that is really satisfying. That's why many of our holidays leave us with such a good feeling inside.

Lots of holidays Americans celebrate have some built-in fun in them, like Hallowe'en, Thanksgiving and New Year. But there's something special about the Jewish holidays. For one, they're ours, they were created by Jews and we observe them because we are Jews. We can even say it the other way too— we are Jews in part because we observe the holidays. After all, they came down to us from our people long ago, and in celebrating them we are following in their tradition.

All through our history our people believed that there was a close and special relationship between them and God, and that one of the things that bound them together was the Torah, which described the way of life by which the Jews were to try to live. Our forefathers therefore took to heart the festivals that were commanded them in the Torah. But they also liked to celebrate other festivals that were not in the Torah, like Chanukah and Purim, because they reminded them of important and stirring events in their long history as a living people.

We are even developing a new festival today, Yom Haatzmaut, not simply because it stands for the birth of the country Israel, but

The Torah decked in all its glory.

more importantly, because it represents a linking up between our ancient and modern history. It was in ancient Palestine that our people became a nation, with their own land and their own rulers. But a long time ago we lost the right to rule ourselves and then, later on, we lost our land too and were forced to settle in various other parts of the world. Now, however, some two thousand years later, a substantial part of our people are living once again on the ancient Jewish soil; once again, a part of our people are ruling themselves in their own country. And so the rest of the Jews, the ten million who do not live in Israel, join with the Israelis to celebrate their Day of Independence, for it is a happy reminder of the continuation of Jewish life on the soil where our history began.

Our holidays lived in the hearts of our people for other reasons besides the fact that they had religious and historical meanings. Our people grew to love them and to look forward to them also, because they introduced colorful customs and practices into their everyday lives, and made the year so much more interesting.

Every holiday brought something special, a different mood, a chance to dress up or to have a change in one's diet. The year, it is true, started on a solemn note; nevertheless, Rosh Hashanah and Yom Kippur did touch the soul, and left people refreshed. And within a few days came Sukkot, bringing with it the joy of harvest and a mood of thanksgiving. A few days later brought festive Simchat Torah and its gladness of spirit, expressed through joyous processions with the Torah and, in some places, dancing in the streets.

This was topped some months later by Chanukah, with its gay songs, delightful observances and games, and memorable lessons. Purim was a time of high spirits, of pure fun and play-acting and song and dance, which was followed a month later by Pesach, with its hallowed customs and important teachings. And seven weeks later the people greeted Shavuot, rejoicing both in the harvest and in the giving of the Torah.

To those in the know, just mentioning the names of the holiday gives the year an air of excitement. They spell out the anticipation of pleasurable activity in the home and in the synagogue.

It has always been the belief among Jews that the more we learn about our religion, and the more we seek to do what the Torah teaches, the deeper will be our appreciation of life. PATHWAYS THROUGH THE JEWISH HOLIDAYS was written in the hope that it will increase your knowledge of the festivals. We hope that it will add to the pleasure you receive as you observe and celebrate the *Yom Tovim*.

PHOTOGRAPHIC CREDITS

American Friends of the Hebrew University, 104

British Museum, Courtesy of the Trustees of the, 41, 61, 62

Israel Office of Information, 13, 22, 27, 29, 35, 46, 47, 49, 54, 56, 76, 84, 85, 90, 91, 92, 99, 102, 107, 125, 129, 133

Jewish Museum, New York, 17, 18, 19, 23, 29, 30, 31, 43, 51, 65, 66, 67, 77, 78, 79, 80, 104, 106, 110, 112, 113, 114, 115, 117, 118

Jewish Theological Seminary, New York, 32, 69

Jewish Welfare Board, New York, 33, 46, 57, 81, 124, 128, 129

Matson Photo Service, The, Alhambra, Calif., 29, 46, 48, 96, 103

Oriental Institute, University of Chicago, 74

Scharfstein, Joel, 5, 27, 88, 93

Seymour, Maurice, 21, 34, 42, 83, 105, 114, 116

Sonnenfeld, Herbert, 20, 33, 74, 81, 82, 117

Sturm, Edward, 48

Union of American Hebrew Congregations, 20, 21, 32, 34, 44, 45, 70, 83, 105, 115

Yale University Art Gallery, 63

YIVO, Yiddish Institute for Jewish Research, 77, 123

Zionist Archives, New York, 12, 26, 31, 47, 55, 89, 98, 106, 122

We have made every effort to identify the sources for all the photographs in this book. If anyone has information about any photographs that have not been identified we will be glad to list them in the next edition.

135

INDEX

A

Abraham, God's promise to,	123
Achad Ha-am	115
Adams, John	85
Adar	14, 67, 118
Adloyadas	67, 69
Afikoman	79, 81, 83
Agag	65
Agricultural festivals, ancient times,	54, 96, 102, 103, 104, 107
see also Harvest festivals	
Ahasuerus	60-64, 66
Akdamut Milin (song)	104-105
Akiba, Rabbi	96, 98
Al chet schechatanu prayer	21
Alexander the Great	39
Aliyah, first, Reform Religious Schools	34
"All the Vows" prayer	18
Amalek	65, 119
America:	
anti-Semitism	89
Chanukah celebration	44-46
Christmas celebration	45
Haggadot,	80, 84-85
modern religious observances	19-21
New World settlers	88
Passover celebration	80-83
Purim celebration	69-70
Sukkot observance	32-34
Tu Bish'vat observance	56
American holidays	5-7
American Indians	84
American Revolution	85
"America's Moses"	85
An Only Kid song,	83
Ani Ma-amin song,	129
Animals, day of rest for	111
Antiochus IV	39, 40, 46, 47
Apocrypha	42
Arabs, in Palestine	89, 90, 93
Aravah	28, 33
Arba kushiot	79
Arch of Titus, Rome	51
Archangel Gabriel	18
Ark	32, 34
Armistice Day	8
Av, 9th day of	122-125
see slso Tishah B'av	

B

Babylon, Jewish captivity	112, 123
Babylon, New Year	10
Babylonians, destruction of Temple by	122
Balfour Declaration	89
Bar Kochba	97
Bar Mitzvah	106
Bat Mitzvah	106
"Before the Words" (song)	104-105
Bet Hamidrash	104
Bazalel Art School menorah, Israel	50
Bialik, Chaim Nachman	118
Bible	5, 22, 42, 70, 88, 104
see also particular books, e.g., Deuteronomy; Esther; etc.	
Bikkurim pageant	107
Bitter herbs	82
B'nei Israel	42
Bokhar Quarter, Israel, Simchat Torah celebration	35
Bokser	56
Booths, and Sukkot observance	27-28, 30
B'reshit, word	118
British Empire	85, 89-90, 92
B'shalach	118

136

C

Calendars	11-15, 19-20, 119
Candle lighting:	
Chanukah	38, 43
Havdalah ceremoney	113, 114
the Sabbath	113, 114
Card games, Chanukah	44
Carnival atmosphere, Purim	67, 68
Carob trees	56
Casting lots	62
Caucasus, Jews from, Purim celebration	69
Chad Gadya	83
Chag Habikkurim	102
see also *Shavuot*	
Chag Hakatzir	102
see also *Shavuot*	
Challah	113, 114
Chametz	76, 78, 79
Chamishah Asar	55
Chanukah	38-52, 60, 119, 132, 133
American observance	44-46
background	38-42
candle lighting	38, 43, 46
card games	44
Christmas influence	45
customs, growth of	42-44
draydl game	43-44, 46, 47
Eastern Europe observance	43-44
gelt	44, 45
Israel observance	46-50
latkes	43, 46, 47
length of celebration	41
menorahs	43, 50, 51
songs	44
Temple dedication	41, 42
Chanukah Oy Chanukah (song)	44
Chanukiyah	50, 51
see also Menorahs	
Charoset	78-79, 82
Chazon, word	123
Cheder, Passover holiday	79
Chinese-Americans	6, 10
Chinese calendar	12
Children's festival, *Tu Bish'vat*	54-58
Christ, word	12
Christianity:	
calendar	11-12
Christmas holiday	45, 46
day of rest	111
Lenten fast	6
Messiah	45
Citron (*etrog*)	28, 30, 33, 35
Colonial America, Passover influence in	85
Columbus Day	7
Communal *seders*	80
Confirmation ceremony	105-106, 107
Consecration ceremony, Reform congregations	34
Conservative Judaism	106, 116
Cyrus	60
Czechoslovakian-Americans	7

D

Dairy dishes, at Shavuot	104
David, House of	105
David, king of Israel	104, 125
Day of Atonement see *Yom Kippur*	
Day of Independence, State of Israel see *Yom Haatzmaut*	
Day of Judgment	18
Day of Remembrance	128-129
Dayenu	82
De Nijis, Judith	35
Declaration of Independence, America,	11, 12
Democracy, and the Sabbath	110-112
Desert walking trips, Israel	49
Deuteronomy, Book of	32, 34, 65
Draydl game	43-44, 46, 47
Drinking, Purim	67

E

Eastern Europe:	
Chanukah	43-44
High Holy Days	16-19
Lag BaOmer	97
Orthodox religious forms	20
Passover	77-80
Purim	64-67
Sabbath	114
Sukkot	30-32
Egypt:	
exodus from	31-32, 65, 73-75, 76, 110, 118, 119
Hebrews in	73-75, 76
New Year	10
special Purim	64
Eighth day of assembly	27
Ein Geb, Israel	35
Einstein, Albert	4
Elijah the Prophet, at Passover	79, 83, 129
Eliyahu Hanavi	129
Elul	19
England	7
see also British Empire	
Equality, idea of	75, 84-85
Erev Shabbat service	116
see also Sabbath	

137

Esther	60-64, 65, 66, 68
Esther, Book of	60-63, 69
Ethiopia	42
Etrog	28, 30, 33, 35
Europe, persecution of Jews	89, 128-129
see also Eastern Europe	
Exodus, Book of	114, 118
Exodus, from Egypt	31-32, 65, 73-75, 76, 110, 118, 119
Ezra the Scribe	112

F

Falashas	42
Fasting:	
of Esther	65
Tishah B'av	122, 124
Yom Kippur	16, 18, 21
Feast of Weeks *see* Shavuot	
Festival of the First Fruits	102
see also Shavuot	
Festival of the Grain Harvest	102
see also Shavuot	
Festival of lights, ancient times	43
see also *Chanukah*	
First amendment, U. S. Constitution	45
First *aliyah*, Reform Religious Schools	34
Flowers, in honor of Sabbath	117-118
Forests, replanting, in State of Israel	56-57
Four questions, Passover	79, 81-82
14th of Adar *see* Purim	
Fourth Commandment	110
see also Sabbath	
Frankfurt, Germany, special *Purim*	64
Franklin, Benjamin	85
Freedom, idea of	75, 84-85
Freedom of religion	45
French-Americans	6
Friday, as day of rest	111
Friday night services	116
see also Sabbath	

G

Gabriel	18
Genesis, Book of	32, 34, 118
George III, king of England	85
German-Americans	6
Germany	7, 128-129
see also Nazism	
Ghettos, Sabbath observance in,	115, 116, 117
Girls, Confirmation for	106
Giving of the Law	103, 105-106
see also Shavuot	
Great Britain *see* British Empire	
Great Sabbath	119
see also Sabbath	
Great Synagogue, Tel Aviv	50
Greece, ancient	111
Greek culture, and Judaism	39-40
Greek-Syrian oppression	42
Greggers	66, 69
Guerrilla resistance fighters, ancient Jerusalem	40

H

Ha-am, Achad	115
Hadar Ha-Carmel, National Religious Party	35
Hadassah	28, 33
Hadrian	96
Haftarah	65, 113, 119, 123
Haggadot	79-80, 81, 82
in America	80, 84-85
newly written	84-85
Reform Judaism changes	80
special prayer for Nazi victims	129
Haifa, Simchat Torah celebration	35
Haifa, Yom Haatzmaut celebration	92
Haifa City Symphony Orchestra	92
Hakafot	34, 35
Hallowe'en	132
Haman	61-64, 65, 66, 69-70
Hamantashn	65, 66, 69
Hanerot Hallalu	44
Harvest festivals	11, 26-36, 75-76, 96-100, 102, 107
Havdalah ceremony	113-114
see also Sabbath	
Hebrew Bible *see* Bible	
Hebrew language	88
Hebrew months, order of	14-15
Hebrew New Year	10, 11, 14-15
see also *Rosh Hashanah*	
Hebrew University	90
Hebrews, in ancient Egypt	73-75, 76
Hellenism	39-40
Herzl, Theodor, Tomb of	91
High Holy Days *see Rosh Hashanah; Yom Kippur*	
High Priest, as Jewish representative	38
High Priest, Temple of Solomon	15-16, 19
Hillel, Rabbi	28, 43
Hitler	89, 90, 128-129
Holidays, American	5-7
Holidays, changes in	7-8
"Holy of Holies," Temple of Solomon	16, 19
Hosea	119
Hoshanah Rabba	31
House of David	105
House of Jacob	73
Housewives, and Sabbath	111
see also Sabbath	

138

I

"I Believe" (song)	129
Idol worship	39-40, 42
Independence Day, America	5, 7, 11
Independence Day, State of Israel	11, 90-93, 129, 132-133
India, B'nei Israel	42
India, *Tu Bish'vat*	56
Indians, American	84
Iran	60
Iranian Jews, Purim celebration	69
Irish-Americans	5-6
Isaiah	123
Israel, State of:	
and Arab countries	46
Chanukah celebration	46-50
creation of	89-90
Day of Independence (*Yom Haatzmaut*)	11, 90-93, 133
High Holiday observance	21-23
Lag BaOmer	97-98
length of Jewish holidays	22
memorial museum for the Six Million	129
menorah as symbol of	50-51
military might	92-93
Passover celebration	22, 83-85
Purim	67-69
Sabbath in	116, 117-118
Shavuot in	107
Simchat Torah celebration	35
Sukkot celebration	34-35
Tishah B'av	124-125
tree planting	56-57
Tu Bish'vat	55-56
War of Independence	90
Yom Hazicaron	129
Israel Prizes, Yom Haatzmaut celebration	92
Israeli *draydl*	47
Italian-Americans	6
Iyar, 4th day of	129
Iyar the 5th	90

J

Jacob	73
Jan Hus Day	7
Jason	39
Jeffeson, Thomas	85
Jeremiah	123-124
Jerusalem, ancient:	
Passover celebration	76-77
Sabbath celebration	112
Sukkot observance	28-30
Temple destruction	122, 124
Jerusalem, modern:	
menorah	50
New Year observance	22
Purim celebration	68-69
return to	88
Simchat Torah celebration	35
Yom Haatzmaut celebration	90-91
Jesus	11-12, 45, 70
Jewish Agency building menorah, Jerusalem	50
Jewish calendar	11-15
Jewish holidays, length of	22
Jewish National Fund, tree planting	55, 56, 57
Jordan, State of	125
Joseph	73
Joshua (Jason), High Priest	39
Judah, Kingdom of	123
Judah Maccabee	40, 41, 42
Judaism, and Hellenism	39-40
Judea	51
Judgment, Book of	19
Julius Caesar	11-12

K

Kaiser Wilhelm, Germany	7
Karaites	112
Kesef, Israel	50
Kibbutzim	107
Purim celebrations	69
special Haggadot	84
Shavuot celebration	107
Sukkot observance	35
Kislev	38, 41, 43
Kiddush	113, 117
Kol Nidre prayer	18, 21, 23
Kreplach	65
Kurdish Jews, *Purim* celebration	69

L

Labor Day	7
Lag BaOmer:	
in East Europe	97
in State of Israel	97-98
in Western countries today	99
Lake Kinneret	35
Lamentations, Book of	123-124
"Land of milk and honey"	88
Latkes, Chanukah	43, 46, 47
Lenten fast, Christians	6
Lincoln's Birthday	7
Los Angeles, California	6
Lulav	28, 33, 35
Lunar calendars	13-14
Lunar month	13

M

Maccabee Sports Club, Israel	47-48
Maccabbes	40, 43, 44, 46, 47, 90
see also Chanukah	
Maccabees, Books of the	42
Maftir	65
Maimonides	129
Maoz Tsur (song)	44
Mardi Gras	6, 67
Maror	82
Masada	47
Mattathias	40
Matzah	76, 78, 79, 81, 82
Megillah readings, *Purim*	60-63, 66, 69
Megillat Esther	60-63, 66, 69
Memorial prayers	21, 34
Menorahs	43, 50, 51
Meron, pilgrimages to	97
Messiah	12, 45, 83, 129
Mexican-Americans	6
Mexican Independence Day	6
Mi Y'mallel	44
Micah, Book of	18
"Model" *seders*	80
Modi'in	40, 47
Mohammed	12
Mohammedans:	
calendar	12, 13
day of rest	111
New Year	10
Moon calendars	13-14, 19-20, 119
Mordecai	61-64
Moses	27, 32, 70, 73-75, 84
	103, 105, 106, 118
Mount Sinai	32, 74, 103, 106
Mount Zion	91, 124, 125
Mt. Zion, "Peace Pilgrimage"	35
"Mummers," Purim festival	68
Myrtle	28, 33

N

Narbonne, special *Purim*	64
National holidays	5-8
National Religious Party, Hadar Ha-Carmel	35
Nature festival, and Passover	75
Nazism	89, 90, 128-129
Nebuchadnezzar	123
Negroes	84
Nehemiah	112
Ner Tamid	41
Nes Gadol Haya Sham	43
Neshef, Israel	48-49
New Orleans, Mardi Gras	6, 67

New World settlers	88
"New Year of the Trees"	54-58
see also *Tu Bish'vat*	
New Years:	
American	132
ancient times	10-11, 15
Chinese	6, 10
Jewish	10, 11, 14-15
see also *Rosh Hashanah*; *Yom Kippur*	
Mohammedan	10
Persian Jews	23
Russian	10
New York City	5-6, 7, 93
N'ila	19, 21
Nile River	10
Nisan	15
Nisan the 15th see Passover	

O

Omer	96
Orthodox Judaism see also Eastern Europe	
religious forms	20
Rosh Hashanah observance	20
and the Sabbath	116
State of Israel, *Simchat Torah* celebration	35
State of Israel, *Yom Kippur* observance	22-23

P

Palestine, ancient:	
Hebrew calendar	13
as Jewish nation	133
New Year	11
promise of return to	123
under Persian Empire	38-39
under Syrian-Greek rule	39-40
Palestine, modern (See also Israel, State of)	
and British Empire	89-90, 92
illegal immigration into	92
Jewish resettlement	88-90
and United Nations	89, 90
Palm branch	28, 29, 33
Pantilat, Jair	47
Passover (*Pesach*):	
in America	80-83
background	73-76
as early American influence	85
Eastern Europe	77-80
and Elijah the Prophet	79, 83, 129
four questions	79, 81-82
Haggadah	79-80, 81, 82, 84-85, 129
length of celebration	22

looking back on	134
Reform Judaism celebration	80-83
seder	76, 77-83
songs	82, 83
special prayer for Nazi victims	129
special Sabbath	119
as spring festival	75-76
State of Israel observance	22, 83-85
Temple times	76
"Peace Pilgrimage," to Mt. Zion	35
Persia, New Year	10
Persian Empire	38-39, 60-64
Persian Jews, Yom Kippur observance	23
Pesach see Passover	
Pharaohs, Egypt	73-74
Pilgrims, Colonial America	85
Pogroms, Europe	89
Prague, special *Purim*	64
"Princess Sabbath"	113
see also Sabbath	
Prophets, Books of the	113
Proverbs, Book of	113
Psalms, *Yom Kippur*	23
Psalms of David	104
Purim:	
adloyadas	67, 69
Christian influence on customs	69-70
drinking	67
Eastern Europe	64-67
hamantashn	65, 66, 69
looking back on	133-134
special Purims	64
special Sabbath	119
State of Israel	67-69
United States	69-70
Purimshpiel	66-67, 69

R

Rain, prayers for	27, 29-30, 33
Red Sea	74
Reform Judaism:	
Chanukah celebration in America	44-46
Confirmation ceremony	105-106, 107
Consecration ceremony, *Sukkot*	34
Haggadah changes	80
Lag BaOmer	99
Passover celebration, America	80-83
Religious Schools	33, 34, 45, 99
Rosh Hashanah observance	20-21
and the Sabbath	116, 117
Shavuot	104-106, 107
Sukkot observance	32-33, 34
Yom Kippur observance	21

Rejoicing in the Law	
see *Simchat Torah*	
Relay race, Chanukah, modern Israel	47
Religion and science	4-5
Religious freedom, first war for	38-42, 45
Religious schools	33, 34, 45, 99
Rest days	110-112
see also Sabbath	
"Return to Palestine"	88
see also Palestine, modern; Israel, State of	
Rhodes, special *Purim*	64
Roasted egg, Passover *seder* symbol	83
Roman Empire:	
Bar Kochba revolt against	97
destruction of Temple by	51, 122-123
disapproval of Sabbath	111
fall of	51
Roman New Year	10-11
Rosh Chodesh blessing	119
Rosh Hashanah:	
American recognition of	7
ancient observance	15, 19-20
background of New Year celebration	10, 11, 15
Eastern Europe	17-18, 20
looking back on	133
Orthodox observance	20
Reform observance	20-21
special Sabbath	119
State of Israel observance	21-23
Temple times	15-16, 19-20
Russian New Year	10
Ruth, Book of	105

S

Sabbath (*Shabbat*):	
in ancient times	112
animals, day of rest for	111
blessing for bread	113
businesses closed	111, 115, 117
candles	113, 114, 117
challah	113, 114
changes in customs and ceremonies	116
Conservative viewpoints	116
cooking	111
day of rest in other religions	111
democracy	110-112
discussion groups	117
Eastern Europe	114
ending of	113-114
Erev Shabbat service	116
in Europe	113, 116
exceptions to rules	112

141

fire and lights	112
flowers	117-118
Fourth Commandment	110
Friday evening ceremony	113, 116, 117
gefilte fish	114
ghetto observance	114, 115, 116-117
Haftarah reading	119
Havdalah ceremony	113-114
housewives	111
Karaites	112
Kiddush	113, 117
law applied to homes	111
meals	111, 113, 114
moon calendar	119
new moon, blessing of	119
Oneg Shabbat	117, 118
Orthodox viewpoints	116
present-day observance	115-117
readings	113, 118
Reform viewpoints	116, 117
rest days	110-112
riding, rules against	116, 117
Rosh Chodesh blessing	119
schools	116
songs	113
special Sabbaths	118-119, 123
in State of Israel	117-118
synagogues	113, 117, 118-119
Talmudic laws	114
Temple of Solomon	112
as time for gladness	112-115
Torah-reading, in synagogues	118
and wealthy people	111
wine	113, 114
work week	110-112
Sabbath of Remembrance	119
Sabbath of Return	119
Sabbath of Shekels	118
Sabbath of Song	118
Sabbath of Vision	123
"St. John's Bread"	56
St. Patrick's Day	5-6
Samuel, Book of	65
Saragossa, special Purim	64
Saul	64, 65
"Scape goat"	16
Scholar's Holiday (*Lag BaOmer*)	96-100
Schools, on Sabbath	116
Science and religion	4-5
Scroll of Esther (*Megillah*)	66
Scrolls of the Law	32, 35
Sea of Galiliee	35
Sea of Reeds	74, 85
Seder	76, 77-83, 88, 129
see also Passover	
Seder, word	79
Seudah, Purim	69
Shabbat see Sabbath	
Shabbat B'reshit	118
Shabbat Chanukah	119
Shabbat Chazon	123
Shabbat Hagadol	119
Shabbat Hamalkah	113
Shabbat Rosh Chodesh	119
Shabbat Shekalim	118
Shabbat Shirah	118
Shabbat Shuvah	119
Shabbat Zachor	119
Shalach manot	66, 69
Shamash	17
Shammai, Rabbi	43
Shavuot:	
Bikkurim pageant	107
changes in	102-103, 107
Confirmation ceremony	105-106, 107
customs attached to	111, 113, 114
as Feast of Weeks	96, 102
food	104
Giving of the Law	103, 105-106
as harvest festival	96, 102, 103, 107
looking back on	134
readings	104-105
Reform Judaism	104-106, 107
songs	104-105, 107
State of Israel	107
Shazar, Zalman	47
Shefa, Gershon	35
Shekel tax	118
Shemini Atzeret	27, 34, 35
Shoah	128-129
Shofar	15, 17-21
Shrove Tuesday	6
Shushan	60, 61
Shuvah, word	119
Sh'vat, month of	55
Sidrah reading	118
Siloam, spring of	29
Simchat Torah (Rejoicing in the Law):	
Consecration ceremony	34
Israel Orthodox Quarter celebration	35
looking back on	113
processions	34, 35
Reform Judaism	34
special Sabbath	118
State of Israel	35
symbolic meaning	32
S'lichot services	17
Simeon Bar Kochba	97
Simeon bar Yochai	96, 97, 98
Sivan, month of	103

Six Million, Day of Remembrance for 128-129
Six Million, memorial museum for 129
Solomon's Temple
   see Temple of Jerusalem
"The Song of Moses" 118
Songs:
   Chanukah 44
   Passover 82, 83, 129
   Sabbath 113
   at *Shavout* 104-105
Spanish-Americans 6
Spring harvest festival 75-76
   see also Harvest festivals
Spring of Siloam 29
State of Israel
   see Israel, State of
Statue of Liberty, New York harbor 5
Sukkah 27-28, 30-31, 32-33, 34
Sukkot:
   American observance 32-34
   ancient times 26-28
   ceremonial dancing, Temple of Solomon 30
   Consecration ceremony, Reform
      congregations 34
   East-European ghetto 30-32
   four symbols 28, 33
   length of observance 34, 35
   looking back on 133
   Reform Judaism 32-33, 34
   State of Israel celebration 34-35
   Temple times 28-30, 42
Sun-time 12-14
Sunday, as day of rest 111
   see also Sabbath
Swimming contest, Israeli 35
Syrian-Greek Empire 39-40, 43, 44

T

Taanit Esther 65
Tallit 123
Talmud, on Sabbath 114
Talmud, at Shavuot 104
Tashlich ceremony 18
Tel Aviv:
   Chanukah relay race 47
   Purim procession 68
   Simchat Torah celebration 35
   tree-planting festival 55
   Yom Haatzmaut celebration 91-92
Temple of Jerusalem:
   destruction of 30, 76, 77, 90, 112, 122-125
   grain offerings to 102
   High Holidays 15-16, 18-19
   rededication of 41, 42

   and Sabbath observation 112
   Syrian-Greek defilement of 39-40
   Sukkot observance 28-30
   tax for 66, 118
   Tishah B'av commemoration 122-125
Ten Commandments 27, 74-75
T'fillin 123
Thanksgiving Day 132
Tiberias, special Purim 64
Tishah B'av:
   fasting 122, 124
   prayers 123
   readings 123-124
   Shabbat Chazon 123
   in State of Israel 124-125
   synagogue services 123, 124
   Temple commemoration 122-125
   tomb of King David, prayers at 125
   Wailing Wall 125
   Zionism 123, 124
Tishri, month of 15, 18, 19, 22, 35
Torah:
   acceptance by people of Israel 74-75, 105
   as binding force 132
   democratic spirit 75, 84
   forbidden by Antiochus 40
   forbidden by Hadrian 96
   given by Moses 32, 74-75, 84, 103, 104, 105, 110, 134
   as Jewish constitution 27, 42
   processions with 32, 34, 35, 133
   Sabbath readings 113, 118
   Simchat Torah readings 32, 34
   Shavuot commemoration 104, 105
   study of 17, 32, 38, 40, 43
Torch-bearing relay race, State of Israel 47
Torchlight processions, *Chanukah*, Israel 49
Travel, High Holidays in Israel 22
Tree certificates, Jewish National Fund 56, 57
Tree planting festival 54-58
Tu Bish'vat (New Year of the Trees):
   agricultural festival, ancient times 54
   children's festival 55-57
   India 56
   Israel 55-56
   United States 56
Turkey, revolt against the Sultan of 64

U

United Nations 89, 90
U.S. Constitution, first amendment 45
Unterman, Yehuda 47

V

Vashti	61
Veterans' Day	7, 8
Vilna, special Purim	64

W

Wailing Wall	125
War of Independence, State of Israel	90
Washington, George	7, 46, 85
Washington's Birthday	7
Water Gate, Temple of Solomon	29
Water ritual, *Sukkot*, Temple times	29
Weizmann, Vera	47
Western calendar	11-12
"Who Knows One?" (song)	83
Wiener, Norbert	4
Willow	28, 29, 30, 33
Working days, and the Sabbath	110-112
World War I	7, 89
World War II	8

Y

Yad Chaim Weizmann	47
Yad Vashem museum, Israel	129
Yemenite community, State of Israel	68
Yemenite Jews, *Purim* celebration	68, 69
Yizkor service	21, 34
Yom Haatzmaut (Independence Day)	90-93, 129, 132-133
Yom Hazicaron	128-129
Yom Kippur:	
American recognition	7
European ghetto	17, 18-19
fasting	16, 18, 21
looking back on	133
Orthodox observance	20, 23
Persian Jews, observance	23
Reform Judaism observance	21
special Sabbath	119
Temple times	15-16, 18-19

Z

Zachor, word	119
Zionism	88-90, 123
Z'man matan toratenu	103
see also *Shavuot*	
Zohar	98